P9-DNQ-134

PERFORMANCE APPRAISAL PHRASE BOOK

The Best Words, Phrases, and Techniques for Performance Reviews

Corey Sandler
and Janice Keefe

Adams Media
Avon, Massachusetts

Copyright ©2004, Word Association, Inc.
All rights reserved. This book, or parts thereof, may not be reproduced
in any form without permission from the publisher; exceptions
are made for brief excerpts used in published reviews.

Portions of this book have been excerpted from *Streetwise® Managing People* and
The Everything® Managing People Book, both copyright ©F+W Media, Inc.

Published by Adams Media, a division of F+W Media, Inc.
57 Littlefield Street, Avon, MA 02322 U.S.A.
www.adamsmedia.com

ISBN 10: 1-58062-940-7
ISBN 13: 978-1-58062-940-9
Printed in the United States of America

30 29 28 27 26 25 24 23 22 21

Library of Congress Cataloging-in-Publication Data
Sandler, Corey
Performance appraisal phrase book / Corey Sandler and Janice Keefe.
p.   cm.
ISBN 1-58062-940-7
1. Employees--Rating of. 2. Performance standards.
I. Keefe, Janice (Janice Jean) II. Title.

HF5549.5.R3S26 2003
658.3'125--dc21

2003004460

This publication is designed to provide accurate and authoritative information
with regard to the subject matter covered. It is sold with the understanding that
the publisher is not engaged in rendering legal, accounting, or other professional advice. If legal advice or other expert assistance is required, the services
of a competent professional person should be sought.
—From a *Declaration of Principles* jointly adopted by a
Committee of the American Bar Association and
a Committee of Publishers and Associations

Many of the designations used by manufacturers and sellers to distinguish
their products are claimed as trademarks. Where those designations appear in
this book and Adams Media was aware of a trademark claim, the designations have been printed with initial capital letters.

*This book is available at quantity discounts for bulk purchases.
For information, call 1-800-289-0963.*

Contents

Introduction

LIFE SEEMS SO VERY SIMPLE when accomplishments can be judged in black and white.

If we're paid for each widget we make, each mile we drive, or each piece of paper we put into a box, we can learn to live—at least on some levels—with our lot in life.

In theory, we know if we can work a little longer or a little harder we can earn a bit more. And we can readily understand that if we don't make enough widgets or drive sufficient miles or pass the required number of papers, we may not be able to hold on to our jobs or receive a promotion or a pay increase.

But for most of us, life is more complicated. We exist in a world that is painted in shades of gray.

What makes a customer service representative a good employee? How do you rate the accomplishments and future job prospects of a corporate trainer? What makes a government or military functionary worthy of an increase in job and pay grade?

The answer: a carefully considered, objective judgment, consistently applied by a qualified supervisor.

The Purpose of an Employee Evaluation

Why do we conduct employee evaluations? It's not because we feel an overwhelming urge to make judgments about others just for the sake of doing so. There are some very specific organizational needs that are fulfilled by a properly conducted evaluation:

- To lay the groundwork for a promotion or salary increase for a star employee
- To attempt to motivate a less-than-stellar performer who has the potential for greater achievement
- To lay the groundwork for the dismissal of an uncooperative, incapable, or otherwise unacceptable worker
- To help a company or agency conduct an inventory of its personnel, in search of ways to improve productivity, reduce redundancy, and find available workers for new assignments

The best reason for an elaborate and careful process for employee evaluations is that it is the right thing to do, guaranteeing everyone a fair deal. The other reason, alas, is that we live in a litigious world, with what seems like a lawyer lurking behind every tree.

The importance of employee evaluations is the establishment of a codified, consistent process to evaluate quantitative and qualitative performance of employees. Properly done, an employer is able to say: "You may not agree with the judgment or be happy with the outcome, but we can prove that every worker is held to the same standard and evaluated in the same way."

Earlier, we defined a proper employee evaluation as a carefully considered, objective judgment, consistently applied by a qualified supervisor.

Let's break down that definition into its components:

Carefully considered. The evaluation has to be based on a thorough and conscientious observation of the employee and work performed.

Objective judgment. There has to be no hint of bias against a particular employee or group of employees.

Consistently applied. The criteria used in the evaluation must be the same for all employees with the same responsibilities.

Qualified supervisor. The evaluator has to be a manager or supervisor with firsthand knowledge of the quality of work performed, and the personal behavior of the employee.

One of the basic rules of procedure at the U.S. Supreme Court is that the justices strive not only to avoid any actual conflicts of interest but also to avoid the appearance of a conflict.

In employee evaluations, the same principle applies: Performance guidelines should not include any subjectivity or the appearance of subjectivity.

The key to proper rating is the establishment of substantial and objective standards and goals.

A performance appraisal is built upon the foundation of a well-crafted job description. The employee is given notice of reasonable expectations and goals, and the supervisor has a framework in place for evaluation.

An overly broad or unreasonably demanding job description is an invitation for trouble, from friction between employee and supervisor up through lawsuits over termination.

Any boss can fire an employee. If you're looking for a script, just watch television sitcoms: "You're fired!" Cue the laugh track; actor exits stage left.

But in the real world, an out-of-the-blue "You're fired!" is more likely to receive a different response: "You'll be hearing from my lawyer," or "I'll take this up with my union steward."

Judgment Calls

We make judgments all the time—first impressions, preferences in clothing and food, and any of the thousands of daily decisions we make about what to do with our lives. We may not like the way someone looks, or the quality of his or her voice, or political opinions. As a man, you might prefer the company of attractive women; a woman might enjoy surrounding herself with handsome men. Most of these judgments are made unconsciously, often based on unexamined experiences, heritage, culture, upbringing, and a bit of genetic code.

Almost none of these highly personal judgments are appropriate subjects for the evaluation of an employee. Stacks of laws and rows of lawyers are lined up to pursue the rights of workers who are in any way judged, compensated, promoted, demoted, or dismissed on the basis of legally irrelevant qualities such as race, religion, or personal beliefs. In most job settings, protected classes also extend to sex and age.

But as a manager or supervisor, your job does include some very important evaluations:

- Is the assigned work being accomplished on schedule?
- Is the product of the expected quality?
- Are all guidelines and rules being followed?
- Has the employee devoted proper attention to training and changes in the industry or sector?
- Is the employee above average, average, or below average in productivity?
- Are tasks properly organized and prioritized?
- Does he or she properly represent the company or organization in dealings with customers, clients, and other agencies or companies?
- Is he or she a candidate for promotion or additional responsibilities?
- Is the employee in need of a strong push to encourage better performance or closer adherence to guidelines and rules? The polite phrase is that the employee needs to be "motivated."
- Is the employee so significantly below expectations that the organization needs to initiate the dismissal process?

About This Book

What do we know about people, jobs, and the English language?

1. People are not machines.
2. Job performance is almost always a judgment call.
3. When it comes to an employee evaluation, all words are not equal.

The purpose of this book is to help you look at the performance of an employee and match your carefully considered judgment with the appropriate objective and consistent words.

Although you could construct a scale with an infinite number of intermediary steps, the basic rating system for employee evaluations divides comments into three tiers:

1. Meets or exceeds standards and goals
2. Needs improvement to meet standards and goals
3. Gives unsatisfactory performance

In this book, you will find thousands of carefully considered phrases, divided into the three tiers.

As a buyer of this book, you are free to use the phrases as presented. However, we expect that in most cases, you'll use these phrases as the starting point for your own statements, adapted as needed to fit your company or agency and the particular employee being evaluated.

Wherever possible, back up your judgment with specific examples. Don't say, "She demonstrates an inability to organize her time," if you can instead say, "She demonstrates an inability to organize her time; for example, in the past quarter she has missed four firm deadlines for submission of critical sales reports while working on tasks of lower priority such as redesigning the color scheme for interoffice memos."

Chapter 1

CAN PERFORMANCE REALLY BE EVALUATED?

As WE NOTED IN THE INTRODUCTION, it would be very nice if every element of job performance could be measured with a scale or a ruler or a counter.

That sort of measurement, of course, works well with a machine. We can gauge the horsepower of an engine, calculate its efficiency, estimate its life expectancy, and then weigh all of its capabilities against the cost of purchase and operation. Accountants can go even further, figuring out the depreciating value of the machine over time. All of these calculations can be precise and objective.

Now consider the evaluation of a human being. Here's one difficult measurement:

Say that an employee's job is to make six widgets in an hour. Counting to six is easy enough, but it's also necessary to determine if they are made correctly. Is there a standard of deviation that's acceptable? If so, is it a precise measurement (each widget can be no more than 0.0032 of an inch larger or smaller than the template), or is it a judgment (each widget feels smooth to the touch and causes no splinters)?

Must the employee complete one widget every ten minutes, or is it okay for the employee to make all six in the lafifteen minutes of each hour? Can the employee make twelve widgets in one hour, then none in the next hour?

Now suppose it's another employee's job to sell six widgets an hour. Is the standard simply sales, or does it factor in returns? What if there are problems with the phone lines or the employee calls forty prospective customers but can't convince any of them to actually buy a widget?

If that wasn't complex enough, suppose we are assigned the task of evaluating a manager who doesn't actually manufacture or sell a product? This person's task, as defined in the job description, is to hire, supervise, and motivate others to make or sell a product or service.

Who is to blame if a supervised employee performs poorly? How far up the line does the credit extend when a staffer demonstrates productivity well above the average or produces work of exceptional quality? And what exactly is the objective definition of quality?

The answer—and it is not a simple or easy one—is that the key to fairness is consistency and impartiality.

This means that employees need to be given a clear and precise definition of what is expected—the job description—and that managers and supervisors must be consistent and fair in judging their employees' fulfillment of expectations.

Think of a job description as the proclamation of expectations. Employees who know what is expected of them can focus their energy on specific goals.

Employers should lay the foundation for good performance immediately after an employee is hired. As part of the initial company orientation, set aside a specific time to review the job description. During this time frame, the supervisor and the new employee should review the details of the job description to ensure a clear understanding of the objectives of the position.

Later on, managers should refer back to the job description in helping struggling or underachieving employees improve their performance.

The supervisor should explain the level of productivity needed and expected and ask the employee, "How long will it take you to reach this level of productivity?" The supervisor should also ask the employee, "What will you need from me to help you reach this level of productivity?" With these simple questions, the supervisor has given the employee the opportunity to set the level of performance at the onset. By giving the employee the power to make this decision, the supervisor has a greater chance of having the employee achieve the performance expectations desired.

Choose Your Words

Before you say a word—or put it in writing—stop and think about the impact of your language.

A written employee evaluation puts you on record, helping you substantiate your actions: promotions, reassignments, discipline, and dismissal. In military/government parlance, it's a CYA situation: Let's translate that as "covering your posterior with paper." At the same time, the recipient can keep your words forever, refer to the written evaluation many times, and share it with a lawyer or a union representative.

For these reasons, you should take every opportunity to consider your words carefully, reviewing them for appropriateness, accuracy, clarity, and the proper tone.

Many human resources experts suggest that an employee

evaluation session be limited to a review of the written report you have prepared. Read aloud your comments and your conclusion, and then listen carefully—and take notes as appropriate—on any responses from the employee. Do not seek to explain or amplify your written comments.

Think about the Game

Before you sit down to compose an evaluation, make a few general notes of your own. Begin by thinking about the overall contributions and capabilities of the employee. Make a careful judgment about whether he or she is:

A Superstar. This is an extraordinary employee who delivers outstanding performance. He or she is exceptional in performance and potential, meeting and exceeding job requirements. When this player comes up to bat, you know your team will receive first-class effort and skill. Your evaluation is intended to praise, reward, and keep him or her in the organization.

An Up-and-Comer. An above-average worker worth keeping and encouraging. The goal here is to take a rookie or a seasoned veteran up a notch to Superstar status.

A Benchwarmer. An average employee, one who fully meets job requirements with work of good quality. They are not the stars, but they are ready, willing, and able to deliver performance good enough to justify a continued paycheck. In sports, many coaches rely heavily on the "bench" to fill in unexpected gaps; the players who sit and wait, though, are easily pushed aside by Up-and-Comers. An employee evaluation of a

Benchwarmer conveys approval, along with suggestions for improvement to get them out of the middle and into the indispensable ranks of Up-and-Comers and Superstars.

Most workers fall into the average category. If they don't, you need to readjust your categories to find the median point.

A Weak Link. A below-average employee, in urgent need of improvement, either because he or she fails to meet job requirements or has violated guidelines. You don't want to hang the future of your team from a Weak Link. Sometimes, though, there are indications of strength or talent worth encouraging and developing.

Headed for the Door. With performance that is not acceptable, this employee is a candidate for dismissal. The evaluation may list specific goals that must be accomplished in order for the worker to hold on to a job, or the evaluation may lay the groundwork for termination.

Once you have thought about the accomplishments and potential of the person you are evaluating, consider what you know about his or her nature and temperament. Is he or she:

- Defensive or cooperative?
- Argumentative or compliant?
- Willing to deal with problems or resistant to any change no matter how worthy?

Finally, consider what specific acts or omissions you can point to as examples to support your judgments. Your position is much stronger—in matters of discipline or reward—if you can relate your judgments to actual performance.

For someone who meets or exceeds expectations, an unsupported statement of praise might read:

"Deals well with unexpected deadlines and stress."

Consider instead the same statement presented with a case in point:

"Deals well with unexpected deadlines and stress, as demonstrated in July of this year when he worked through the weekend to prepare an emergency shipment of customized widgets for the Wintergreen Company, an important client."

For an employee who needs improvement:

"Must become better able to deal with unexpected deadlines and stress; as an example, the emergency order of customized widgets for the Wintergreen Company in July of this year required intervention and assistance from senior management for completion."

And for an employee who delivers unsatisfactory performance:

"Does not deal well with unexpected deadlines and stress. As an example, the emergency order of customized widgets for the Wintergreen Company in July of this year was not fulfilled on time for the customer, and the product that was shipped did not meet our standards of quality."

A Spectrum of Judgment

The various Eskimo and Inuit languages are supposed to have several dozen words to describe slightly different types of snow. By that line of thinking, we can certainly afford to expand our vocabulary when it comes to adjectives.

Good, satisfactory, acceptable, and *adequate* all can be fairly used to describe someone whose performance is up to standards. But there are small degrees of difference between them; most of us would prefer to have our performance described as "good" rather than "adequate."

Consider the following spectrum of adjectives that span the spread from extraordinary to unacceptable. You can add your own descriptors to the scale. One way to use the list: Assign a numerical value to an employee's attributes on a scale from 1 (the weakest) to 20 (the strongest) and select appropriate adjectives in and about that number.

Extraordinary

extraordinary:
marvelous; remarkable; superlative; surprising; wonderful

exceptional:
great; incomparable; matchless; notable; noteworthy; unequaled; unique; unmatched; unsurpassed; significant; special; striking

excellent:
admirable; brilliant; first-rate

outstanding:
remarkable; significant; terrific

Above Average

exemplary:
creditable; laudable; praiseworthy

superior:
accomplished; commendable; consummate; expert; high quality; skilled

very good:
estimable; highly regarded; impressive; worthy

more than adequate:
fine; more than sufficient; more than ample

Acceptable

good:
decent; good quality; respectable; skillful

satisfactory:
appropriate; apt; fitting; proper

acceptable:
good enough; okay; up to standard

adequate:
allowable; passable; reasonable; tolerable

Below Average

fair:
barely adequate; fair to middling

poor:
inferior; meager; weak

less than adequate:
inadequate; insufficient; paltry; scant; derisory

minimal:
insignificant; negligible; slight; token; trifling; trivial

Unacceptable

unsatisfactory:
beneath standard; inferior; low-grade; mediocre; poor quality; second-rate; substandard

undependable:
devious; not to be trusted; unstable; untrustworthy

unreliable:
changeable; erratic; fickle; not to be relied upon; unpredictable; variable

unacceptable:
insufficient; intolerable; objectionable

Chapter 2

INSIDER TIPS FOR EMPLOYEE EVALUATION

THE KEY TO THE PROPER CONDUCT of an employee evaluation is this: Evaluate the performance, not the person.

It is improper, ineffective, and sometimes illegal to base your judgment on the personal characteristics of an employee. It doesn't matter what they think or believe, whether they mean well or not, or whether they have a winning personality or a loser's attitude—unless and until these attributes affect their performance on the job.

Put another way, if you find fault, blame the action or the method or the planning, but not the person.

Focus on the Specific and Observable

If you or someone else didn't observe it, it didn't happen—at least for the purposes of an employee evaluation. This is not a meeting about feelings or suspicions. It is about actions and behaviors you can see, hear, or are otherwise tangible—work that didn't get done, assignments done incorrectly, inappropriate e-mail messages, and so on—that reflect on the performance of this employee.

Have examples such as the following.

"Here is the memo you sent to accounts receivable about the Robinson account. It has the wrong balances, and you erroneously flagged the account as past due."

"I've gotten complaints from other departments about the number of off-color jokes you forward by e-mail. Here are copies of messages that people have given me."

"When we established the timeline for the widgets, you agreed that it was reasonable and would accommodate the kinds of delays that might arise. I've checked with you every week, and you've said you had everything under control. The widget prototype still isn't to manufacturing, though the timeline says it should have been in full production six weeks ago."

What about a "Bad Attitude"?

You might see the crux of the problem as attitude, and that could indeed be the case. But you still need tangible evidence—and usually there's an abundance of it: yelling at coworkers, badmouthing others, showing up late, and leaving early. Provide a few examples:

"On Tuesday you came in at 9:30 A.M. and you weren't at your desk after 2:30 P.M. On Thursday, you got here at 11 A.M. and I watched you leave at 3:15 P.M."

"Monday at lunch you were overheard saying that the Mitchell project was nothing but a joke and if this company had any smarts it would fire the whole team."

Unless you've asked other employees if you can identify them when talking to the problem employee, don't name names. Keep the conversation focused on the employee who is in the room with you, and on behaviors rather than personalities. Explain why the behaviors are problems, just to be sure you and the employee have the same understanding (which is not to imply that you must agree).

Maintain Control

Like it or not, when it comes to an employee evaluation, you are supposed to be in charge. You are representing your company, department, or agency in an important personnel matter. The best way to keep control of the meeting is to come through the door with a plan, and to stick to it.

Here are some suggestions:

Establish ground rules. Say, "I will tell you my assessment of your performance for each measurement, and then give you an opportunity to share your perspectives and comments. I ask that you not interrupt me, and I promise I won't interrupt you."

Stay focused on the topics at hand and keep digressions to a minimum. Present examples of observable behaviors to support your comments. If issues surface that warrant further discussion, schedule another appointment to address them.

Take notes, and encourage the employee to do the same. Remember that the employee evaluation has a goal: to reward and encourage a worthy worker, to prod an underachiever, or to give a hard push to a member of the staff delivering an unacceptable performance. Anything you say to an employee should reinforce your written comments, and anything said in response should be noted as evidence of cooperation or resistance.

Present improvements from a positive perspective as much as possible. "You've done a great job developing a system for monitoring report status. Let's take a look at some ways that you can streamline your work flow to be more efficient."

If there is bad news, it shouldn't be news to the employee. He or she should know, or at least suspect, that there is a problem; if not, you have failed to do a proper job of communicating with your staff. Be direct in presenting the problem, and have a sense of what action you intend to take in response.

Involve the employee in developing an improvement plan. Specifically identify steps and measures as well as a timeline for change.

Offer the employee the opportunity to add his or her comments (if your company or agency policy permits). Responses are usually included on a separate page in the evaluation packet that becomes part of the employee's file.

How to Schedule an Evaluation

How many times have you said something in the heat of the moment that you wished you could erase from everyone's memory? Are you supremely confident in your ability to stick to the script, no matter what response you receive from a belligerent employee? How clear are you in your own mind about the outcome you expect from an employee evaluation session?

The answers you gave, we're sure, are not all that reassuring. But they are quite common: Very few of us are very good at off-the-cuff, unprepared formal encounters. That's the bad news; the good news is that there is no reason not to make yourself prepared for effective employee evaluations.

Here are some guidelines on the best way to schedule an evaluation:

- Meet only when you are certain you can remain calm and professional. If you're angry because the employee's problems have caused your superiors to come down on you, give yourself a day or two to cool off.
- Meet someplace that ensures privacy. If your office is not appropriate, meet in a conference room or borrow someone else's workplace.
- Have a clear agenda of what you want to cover, and put it in writing if that will help you stay on track.
- Have documentation of the problems you want to discuss—notes, memos, copies of e-mail, work that had to be redone, or whatever other evidence is relevant. Be discreet, of course—have the items in a file folder, not spread out on the desk when the employee arrives.
- Know, at least in general, what you want the employee to do to remedy the situation.

Ten Insider Tips for Employee Evaluation

When in doubt, and especially when you are not in doubt, tell the truth. That's a great starting position for the upright conduct of any employee evaluation.

But before you say a word, do your homework. Know what you want to say, why you want to say it, and make a carefully considered decision on how to present your case.

In most companies, organizations, and agencies, you should consult with your human resources department or supervisor for specific instructions and advice.

Here is a valuable collection of insider tips for giving an accurate and truthful evaluation:

1. *Start with a carefully crafted job description.* Make certain the employee is given a copy when offered a job and any time a promotion or reassignment is made. The evaluation measures performance against the job description.

2. *Ask the employee to complete a self-evaluation before the review session.* This asks employees to think about their own performance and role in the enterprise.

If you have consistently offered both praise and constructive criticism during the previous year, the employee should have a good idea of where he or she stands, which should help open the lines of communication for the performance appraisal itself.

Ask for the self-evaluation a day or so ahead of the performance review. Read the employee's comments carefully to gain a sense of whether the worker has a realistic view of his or her performance, whether there are any issues they may have that you did not anticipate discussing, and whether you may expect a defensive, belligerent, or uncooperative attitude.

The best possible outcome: You open the performance appraisal by noting your agreement with the employee's self-evaluation. You offer praise and interest, and most importantly, you work together with the employee to put together a plan to improve performance, productivity, and other issues.

The second-best outcome: You come into the performance appraisal session knowing some or all of the employee's concerns and issues, and you are prepared to deal with them.

3. *Plan your opening statement.* A valued employee should hear praise and positive comments at the start, before you move on to constructive criticism.

A weak or below-average employee, and especially a worker on the track to termination, should get the carefully phrased criticism up-front and carefully delineated. Why? Because many people under stress will focus on any words of praise to filter out things they don't want to hear.

4. *Be objective in your evaluation and consistent in your judgments.* Refer to specific incidents in your evaluation. Take notes when an employee describes an exemplary—or condemnable—act.

Keep personality conflicts and your personal biases out of the review.

5. *When possible and appropriate, use measurable criteria.* If you have previously told an employee you expected an increase in sales of 20 percent, produce the numbers to back up your comments—positive or negative.

If at an earlier performance evaluation, you asked for a change in behavior, such as maintaining a friendly demeanor when answering the phone, provide an assessment of progress or lack or progress on that specific issue.

6. *Separate the salary review from the performance review.* (One exception: If you are rewarding an employee with an above-average evaluation with an above-average raise.) Tell the worker you want to discuss his performance and ways to help him become an even better member of the team; even if you have already decided on a salary adjustment, schedule a discussion of salary for a later time after you both have had time to consider the results of the performance evaluation. In this way the message of the evaluation does not become overshadowed by the reaction to a change in salary.

7. *Link criticisms to solutions.* Tell your employee your concerns and then offer suggestions to eliminate them.

8. *Don't let the session get out of control.* Stick to the point, refuse to argue, and don't let the employee take command of the review.

9. *Make sure your words are heard.* If you think the employee has tuned you out or does not understand, ask her to paraphrase your comments back to you.

You can do the same when you receive unclear responses: "Let me see if I understood you correctly. You said . . . "

10. *Have the employee sign the evaluation.* Though he may not agree with any or all of your observations, the signature shows that the employee has received the document. This helps protect you from claims that the worker did not know of specific concerns about performance and attitude.

Step-by-Step Through an Employee Evaluation

Employee evaluations can be stressful and difficult even in the best of situations. As a conscientious and effective supervisor, you are dedicated to helping your company or agency fulfill its mission and at the same time you are committed to fairness and empathy for your staffers and coworkers. There is often a difference in direction between the two goals.

The employee you are evaluating is likely to be tense and sometimes highly defensive. After all, your words are by definition a judgment about her abilities and intent, and to a great extent you are determining her livelihood.

Therefore, one of the most important things you need to do is be prepared with a specific agenda for the evaluation. Know what you plan to say, and stick to the script.

Here are step-by-step suggestions for a well-prepared evaluation session:

Greeting. Start the review with a warm greeting and perhaps some very brief small talk to help relax tensions and create an atmosphere more conducive to the review.

Summary. Be sure that the employee understands exactly how his or her overall performance ranks. Summarize the overall performance first and then explain what the rating means. Don't announce any salary changes at this point. If you don't give the summary at the beginning of the review, the employee will spend the rest of the review trying to figure out your judgment of his or her overall performance, based on your comments.

The employee might want to discuss the rating immediately after you offer it. Put this off until you have reviewed the employee's strengths and weaknesses thoroughly.

Strengths. Unless an employee's performance is unsatisfactory, compliment him or her on both major and minor strengths as they relate to the job. Avoid saying anything negative until you have reviewed his or her strengths. You can either be specific or general in describing strengths.

Weaknesses. Unless an employee's performance has been truly exceptional, you should offer comments on areas of weakness, or at least suggest room for improvement. In reviewing weaknesses, be as specific as possible. For example, rather than saying, "You have a poor attitude," cite a specific example of his or her behavior, such as "You are often late for company meetings and several times throughout the year you complained incessantly about company policies."

Feedback. After you have discussed an employee's weaknesses, you should give that person an opportunity to air his or her thoughts. Listen politely until the person is done. Avoid being argumentative, but do let the employee know that his or her feedback has not affected your review. For example, you may want to say, "I understand that you don't agree with what I have said, but my perception of your overall performance remains as I have stated it."

Closing. Unless the employee's performance is substantially less than satisfactory, try to end the review on a positive note. You might say, "The company and I very much appreciate your work, and we are glad to have you here."

Chapter 3

LEGAL MATTERS

AN EMPLOYER-EMPLOYEE RELATIONSHIP is in some ways like
a marriage—happy and productive when things go well, but
tense and threatening when they don't.

It takes a great deal of tact and careful attention to the
feelings—and rights—of others to encourage a dismissed
employee to exit gracefully. And it takes relatively little to
push someone into a position where they feel it necessary to
hire a lawyer to file suit. (As any lawyer will tell you,
anyone can file a lawsuit whether they have good grounds to
do so or not.)

There are three things you must do to protect yourself
and your company or organization:

1. *Stay within state and federal laws that oversee
employment and dismissal procedures.* Keep current on
employment law, and if possible work closely with a professional human resources manager or attorney. If your company or agency is a party to a collective bargaining
agreement, be sure you follow all of its requirements. Always
involve your human resources department or attorney in any
situation that comes near legal or contractual issues.

2. *Be consistent in your handling of all employees with similar assignments and responsibilities.* Create, update, and use job descriptions as a benchmark to measure performance. Company and organizational policies should be published in a handbook or otherwise readily available for review at any time. Be consistent in procedures for evaluations and salary reviews to affirm fairness and equal treatment for all.

3. *Conduct evaluations as objectively as possible.* Concentrate on performance and acts rather than the personal attributes of the employee. Back up judgments with specific examples wherever possible.

Pitfalls to Avoid

The good news is that very few of us are consciously racist, sexist, ageist, or prejudiced against someone's religious or personal beliefs.

The bad news is that many of us can and do inadvertently stray across the line; the damage that results may be a momentary upset or may lead to a serious legal matter.

Laws and court rulings have established limited situations in which an employer can specify that applicants must be of a particular size, weight, or physical capability; in even more limited circumstances, the employer can exclude someone on the basis of sex. The loopholes are supposed to be limited to bona fide occupational qualifications where a characteristic is a necessary job requirement.

For example, if the job requires lifting ninety-pound sacks of cement, the employer can reject someone unable to perform that act; the requirement must be reasonable and consistently applied to all applicants. A church can in certain circumstances require that an employee be an adherent, and a health club can insist that an attendant in the women's locker room be female. But it is probably not a bona fide occupational requirement that a librarian be a six-foot-tall male or that a sales clerk in a shoe store be a woman.

In any case, the book in your hands deals with evaluations of employees who are already on the payroll, and here the prohibitions against employee discrimination are more clear-cut.

In general, in an employee evaluation (and in most other situations), never refer to an employee's:

- age
- court or legal record
- marital status
- physical disability
- political position
- race
- religion
- sex
- sexual preference
- weight

Unless it is germane to the job or violates properly developed company policy, do not refer to an employee's style of dress or grooming, personal life, or activities conducted in private life.

If you have the slightest shadow of a doubt about the appropriateness of any comment you plan to make as a supervisor, consult with your company's or agency's human resources department or lawyer before you say or write a word.

Performance Review Legal Issues

Sometimes it may seem as if the very act of conducting an employee evaluation is a damned-if-you-do and damned-if-you-don't situation. You fear that the very act of evaluating an employee opens you to a Pandora's Box of legal or collective bargaining agreement disputes. But the failure to conduct an evaluation can damage your company's or agency's ability to meet its goals or maintain an effective and productive workplace.

In some instances, a middle ground—a toothless and meaningless review conducted just for the sake of appearances—can cause problems in both directions: legal challenges for lack of consistency and workplace issues from dissatisfied staff.

The biggest job-related legal problems are often a direct result of unrealistic employment reviews. Managers often avoid conflict by failing to appraise a poor employee performance accurately and truthfully. Later, if the company fires the employee, it is easier for that employee to claim discrimination and offer his or her performance reviews as evidence of adequacy to carry out the job requirements.

1. *Give a realistic review.* So, as a first step, you need to make sure that all managers give each member of their staff a realistic review. Additionally, all reviews should be issued

in writing. The reviewed employee should receive a copy of his or her review.

2. *Develop consistent review criteria.* You might encounter another potential legal pitfall when an employee claims that he or she has been discriminated against in the review. This is particularly likely to occur if the employee has been passed up for a promotion. To avoid this, you need to develop consistent review criteria and be absolutely sure that your managers adhere to the performance criteria. Reviews should also contain specific examples of negative and positive performance, not just generalizations.

3. *Other steps.* Other ways to avoid legal issues during reviews are as follows:

- Establish grievance procedures.
- Have more than one manager determine each employee's overall performance rating or at least provide input during the pre-appraisal process.
- Give employees feedback during the year, as appropriate, to avoid performance review surprises.
- Encourage managers to work with employees who are underachievers in an attempt to raise their performance to a satisfactory level.

Importance of Documenting Poor Performance

Although many managers might be worried that putting negative comments about a worker into writing can end up creating legal problems later on, the reverse is also true: If an employee dismissal is challenged in court, your position is much stronger if there is a paper trail to support the action.

Keep your comments focused on performance, and not on personal attributes. Be as specific as you can about particular events. Make sure that your comments support your actions.

Chapter 4

STRATEGIES FOR DEALING WITH UNSATISFACTORY PERFORMANCE

IN MOST CASES, IT IS IN YOUR BEST INTEREST to attempt to help any employee to improve the quality and quantity of work produced, or to assist the worker in meeting expectations or following company or agency guidelines. It is expensive and disruptive to the organization to pay severance to a terminated employee and then to bear the cost of searching for, hiring, and then training a replacement.

Helping a Below-Average Employee Improve

The first decision, of course, is whether the employee is worth the effort to keep and retrain. In the best of circumstances, the employee evaluation will combine a wake-up call to the substandard worker and a package of suggestions and assistance that will help bring him or her up to the expected level of performance.

The evaluation session begins with a report by the supervisor that voices concerns about performance and productivity, and gives the employee a chance to respond. After the problems are identified, the next step is the development of a plan for improvement.

Although it is valuable to involve the employee in the creation and execution of a plan for improvement, as a supervisor your first obligation is to make sure that the plan seeks to achieve the goals that are important to your company or organization.

Options include additional training through classes or workshops, direct tutoring with a more experienced employee, job-shadowing, a change of responsibilities, a transfer to another department, and other choices.

There are three elements that should be included in any improvement plan:

Specific goals for, and descriptions of, the improvements you want to see. "Memos that leave this department must be free from grammatical and spelling mistakes."

Specific steps for achieving the described improvements. "I want you to run spellchecker just before you save or print any document. For the next two weeks, I want to sit down with you at 11 A.M. and 3 P.M. to review all outgoing memos. We will proof them together."

Specific methods for measuring performance and assessing improvement. "I ran spellchecker on these memos that I showed you, and each had at least seven errors. By the end of one week, I want the memos we review together to have fewer than three errors each. At the end of two weeks, I want every memo we review together to have no errors that spellchecker is capable of detecting. We'll meet again at the end of two weeks to discuss your improvement."

If your words of encouragement and suggestions for improvement don't work, the next step is a warning that sets a specific goal and a deadline. Some experts recommend that the warning be delivered verbally, followed up after a short period of time with a written recap—a one-two punch designed to forcefully grab the employee's attention to the seriousness of the situation.

If encouragement, motivation, and threats don't work, though, there is no point is putting off the inevitable. Working with your human resources department, the time has come to dismiss the underachieving employee.

How to Fire an Employee

Not every employee can be motivated, encouraged, or retrained in a way that allows them to meet or exceed expectations. Sooner or later in most organizations, an employee has to be fired . . . terminated . . . laid off . . . shown the door . . . cashiered . . . dismissed . . . bounced . . . sacked . . . or canned. (We're rather fond of the British euphemism of "made redundant.")

Whatever you call it, a firing is not a pleasant event for the employee or for a caring supervisor. And, in some cases, it is an invitation to a lawsuit; that doesn't mean that every time someone is terminated they hire a lawyer, but as a supervisor you need to take every precaution to make sure you follow the law.

None of this takes away the right of an employer to dismiss a worker for cause—poor performance or behavior, or for demonstrable economic reasons such as downsizing—but companies and organizations need to be prepared to document their reasons.

As you prepare for terminating someone, remember that employees have rights; in general, they cannot be arbitrarily fired and they certainly cannot be dismissed because of their race, sex, or personal beliefs.

The second-most-important point: Carefully document your rationale for dismissal. It is not sufficient to say that an employee "didn't fit in" or "didn't work hard enough." The employee's files, or the employee evaluation, need to list specific instances of substandard or unacceptable performance or behavior.

One piece of documentation that can turn around to bite you: previous employee evaluations that do not show concerns, warnings, and specific demands for improvement or changes in behavior. If the employee's work records show only words of praise, or vague and nonspecific criticism, your position is weak.

How much time should you give an employee to improve performance? There really aren't specific guidelines. One thing to take into consideration, however, is the employee's length of service with your company. Loyalty does count. Give an employee who has served you for several years a few months to work out his or her performance deficits.

Remember, too, that when you fire a long-term employee, the negative effect on the morale of other employees will be far greater than, say, if you were to fire a recent hire. And when you work together with long-term employees in an effort to help them improve their job output, and ideally keep them gainfully employed, you create good will throughout the company.

Chapter 5

QUALITATIVE ATTRIBUTES

HOW SUCCESSFUL IS AN EMPLOYEE at making decisions, demonstrating loyalty to the organization, negotiating a deal, or making a presentation? These are all qualitative attributes that affect performance and productivity.

In your employee evaluation of qualitative attributes, be sure to connect attitudes and skills to specific goals and requirements of the job. In this section, for example, you'll find suggested language that says, "Does not deal well with unexpected deadlines and stress."

Your full evaluation, then, could note that the employee "does not deal well with unexpected deadlines and stress, which are an ordinary part of the activity as defined in the job description. For example, the employee has consistently failed to meet regular deadlines for shipment of new products as noted in the attached report."

- Adaptability to change
- Analytical skills
- Aptitude and competence
- Communication skills
- Creativity
- Decision-making skills

- Dependability and responsibility
- Initiative in accomplishing goals
- Judgment skills
- Logic skills
- Loyalty to the organization
- Motivation to accomplish tasks and goals
- Negotiating skills
- Oral presentation skills
- Persuasion skills
- Presentation skills
- Problem-solving skills
- Professionalism, standards, and ethics
- Quality of work
- Sales skills
- Secretarial and clerical skills
- Self-improvement and learning skills
- Writing skills

Adaptability to Change

Key Verbs

acclimates	deals	shows
adapts	demonstrates	welcomes

Key Nouns

assignments	deadlines	problems
capabilities	demands	procedures
challenges	flexibility	reorganization
change	policies	responsibilities

| resructuring | stress | versatility |
| skills | tasks | |

Meets or Exceeds

- Able to adapt to changes in deadlines and changes in the nature of assignments.
- Able to deal with multiple, competing demands.
- Able to take on new tasks and responsibilities when necessary.
- Ably leads and participates in restructuring and reorganizational committees.
- Acclimates to changes easily.
- Adapts to change very well.
- Adapts well to new policies and reorganization.
- Deals well with reorganization and restructuring.
- Deals well with unexpected deadlines and stress.
- Demonstrates a broad range of skills and capabilities.
- Demonstrates flexibility in adapting to change.
- Is a multitalented individual.
- Is a strong candidate for assignments or promotion.
- Is a very versatile, flexible, and capable worker.
- Is always willing to accept new assignments.
- Is capable of more responsibility and challenges.
- Is open to suggestions and ideas of others.
- Shows initiative in seeking solutions to problems.
- Welcomes constructive change.
- Welcomes the opportunity to take on new responsibilities and challenges.
- Is willing to try new methods.
- Works well with other individuals and departments in dealing with change.

Needs Improvement

- Displays a very limited range of capabilities.
- Must become better able to deal well with unexpected deadlines and stress.
- Must find ways to adapt well to new policies and reorganization.
- Must show willingness to try new methods.
- Needs to be able to take on new tasks and responsibilities when necessary.
- Needs to better adapt to change.
- Needs to demonstrate ability to deal with multiple, competing demands.
- Needs to demonstrate better ability to acclimate to changes.
- Needs to demonstrate capability for more responsibility and challenges.
- Needs to demonstrate flexibility in adapting to change.
- Needs to learn to adapt well to changes in deadlines and changes in the nature of assignments.
- Needs to readily accept change in policies or procedures.
- Should be more willing to accept new assignments.
- Should be more willing to participate in restructuring and reorganizational efforts.
- Should demonstrate an interest in taking on new responsibilities and challenges.
- Should show more initiative in seeking solutions to problems.
- Should strive to be more flexible in performance of work.
- Should strive to demonstrate capability for additional assignments or promotion.

- Should strive to work better with other individuals and departments in dealing with change.
- Should welcome constructive change.
- Should work to better embrace reorganization and restructuring efforts.
- Should work to display a broader range of skills and capabilities.

Unsatisfactory

- Does not adapt well to change.
- Does not adapt well to changes in deadlines and changes in the nature of assignments.
- Does not adapt well to new policies and reorganization.
- Does not deal well with reorganization and restructuring.
- Does not deal well with unexpected deadlines and stress.
- Does not demonstrate versatility and flexibility.
- Does not display a broad range of skills and capabilities.
- Does not readily accept change in policies or procedures.
- Does not show initiative in seeking solutions to problems.
- Does not work well with other individuals and departments in dealing with change.
- Fails to demonstrate flexibility in adapting to change.
- Has not demonstrated candidacy for additional assignments or promotion.
- Has not shown ability to acclimate well to changes.
- Has not shown capability for more responsibility and challenges.
- Has shown inability to deal with multiple, competing demands.
- Is not able to take on new tasks and responsibilities when necessary.

- Is one-dimensional.
- Is unwilling to accept new procedures.
- Is unwilling to try new methods.
- Resists change.
- Resists participation in restructuring and reorganizational efforts.
- Shows a strong lack of interest in taking on new responsibilities and challenges.
- Shows an unwillingness to accept new assignments.

Analytical Skills

Key Verbs

| analyzes | demonstrates | uses |
| applies | displays | utilizes |

Key Nouns

algorithms	logic	statistical models
formulas	methodologies	statistics
information	problems	trends
judgment	problem-solving	

Meets or Exceeds

- Analyzes information and trends with great skill.
- Applies proven methodologies to solve problems.
- Demonstrates excellent skills in analytical reasoning.
- Demonstrates mastery of essential formulas and algorithms.
- Demonstrates understanding of statistical models for problem analysis.

- Effectively uses logic as a problem-solving tool.
- Is a proven problem-solver.
- Is capable of dissecting a problem into manageable parts.
- Is methodical and deliberate.

Needs Improvement

- Does not use good judgment in all situations.
- Lacks the discipline to make careful evaluations.
- Needs to be better able to break down a problem into smaller, manageable parts.
- Needs to develop skills in using methodologies to solve problems.
- Needs to improve analytical skills.
- Needs to improve skills with application of essential formulas and algorithms.
- Needs to improve understanding of statistical models used for problem analysis.

Unsatisfactory

- Does not demonstrate a disciplined mind necessary to make precise judgments.
- Failed to improve skills on problem-solving methodologies.
- Fails to demonstrate adequate analytical skills.
- Has not demonstrated proficiency with the use of essential formulas and algorithms.
- Has proved unable to deal with problems as the sum of many manageable parts.
- Unwilling to undergo training to improve understanding of statistical models used for problem analysis.

Aptitude and Competence

Key Verbs

demonstrates
displays
exhibits
shows

Key Nouns

ability	education	self-confidence
aptitude	expertise	seminars
background	performance	skills
classes	potential	training
competence	proficiency	

Meets or Exceeds

- Attends appropriate seminars and classes to improve capabilities and skills.
- Brings a unique set of skills and background to the job.
- Demonstrates a high degree of specialized skill.
- Demonstrates a high level of competence.
- Devotes a great deal of time to updating skills and job-related education.
- Displays a high degree of self-confidence.
- Exhibits a willingness to work with others to advance knowledge and expertise whenever possible.
- Is proficient and capable.
- Is skillful and talented.
- Makes the most of abilities.
- Shows a high level of expertise in job-related tasks.

Needs Improvement

- Could make more of abilities.
- Is closed-minded about advancing skills through courses or seminars.
- Needs to improve level of competence to meet needs of job.
- Needs to improve level of expertise in job-related tasks.
- Needs to improve skills and capabilities.
- Performs at less than potential.
- Should devote more time and effort to education to improve capabilities and skills.
- Should improve skills in specialized areas.
- Should seek a needed specialized skill.
- Should spend more time updating skills and job-related education.
- Should work to improve self-confidence.

Unsatisfactory

- Does not show a level of skill or competence necessary for the job.
- Does not use abilities to the utmost.
- Does not work to full potential.
- Fails to improve deficiencies in specialized skills.
- Fails to keep current on skills and job-related education.
- Fails to make effort to improve capabilities and skills through education.
- Has failed to demonstrate necessary level of competence.
- Has failed to improve level of expertise in job-related tasks.
- Has made no attempt to improve performance and competency.

- Refuses to take steps to advance level of proficiency.
- Shows a low level of self-confidence, and has failed to take steps to improve competency.

Communication Skills

Key Verbs

applies	cultivates	responds
articulates	delivers	shows
communicates	demonstrates	speaks
contributes	facilitates	
conveys	fosters	

Key Nouns

committee	honesty	mission statement
concepts	ideas	policies
conference calls	image	positions
consensus	information	procedures
corporate mission	instructions	results
credibility	language	spokesperson
e-mail	letters	suggestions
goals	meetings	thoughts
groupware	memos	values

Meets or Exceeds

- Applies the values embodied in the corporate mission statement.
- Articulates positions and concepts well.
- Asks thoughtful and effective questions at meetings.

- Capable of clear and direct communication with others.
- Communicates divisional and company goals with great skill.
- Communicates effectively.
- Communicates effectively with other departments and divisions.
- Communicates effectively within the department.
- Communicates ideas, instructions, and information well.
- Communicates management decisions well.
- Communicates policies and procedures well.
- Communicates the company's mission statement to customers and suppliers.
- Communicates the results of meetings to superiors clearly and concisely.
- Communicates well in interoffice memos.
- Communicates well in (foreign language).
- Communicates well with coworkers at meetings.
- Communicates well with customers and clients.
- Communicates well with superiors and supervisors.
- Communicates well with supervised staff.
- Contributes valuable insight and direction at meetings.
- Conveys a positive image of the company to customers and clients.
- Demonstrates a clear understanding of the corporate mission.
- Demonstrates communication skills at meetings.
- Demonstrates excellent consensus-building strategies.
- Demonstrates excellent skills as a communicator.
- Demonstrates personal credibility and honesty in communication.

- Demonstrates skills in moving undecided meeting participants to consensus.
- Developed new methods to manage teleconferences and conference calls.
- Encourages others to communicate openly and effectively.
- Facilitates meetings with great skill.
- Fosters an open and honest environment for the exchange of ideas.
- Fosters consensus-building at meetings.
- Fosters open communication in groups and meetings.
- Helps facilitate communication at meetings.
- Incorporates the mission statement in important communications.
- Is a skillful orator.
- Is an effective spokesperson.
- Keeps meetings on subject and on schedule.
- Listens well to suggestions and ideas of others.
- Makes effective use of communication technology.
- Makes good use of electronic communication services, including e-mail, groupware, and teleconferencing.
- Manages electronic messages well.
- Manages foreign-language translation of documents with great skill.
- Manages meetings that foster open communication among participants.
- Organizes and manages teleconferences and conference calls well.
- Organizes and runs meetings with skill.
- Oversees electronic communication with great skill.
- Possesses an exceptional vocabulary.

- Properly documents verbal communication when appropriate.
- Responds quickly to all incoming communication.
- Skilled in committee procedure.
- Speaks and reads (foreign language).
- Speaks well.
- Thoughts and instructions are delivered clearly and concisely.
- Works well to implement consensus decisions.
- Works well with others to facilitate communication.

Needs Improvement

- Communications skills need improvement.
- Needs to better communicate divisional and company goals.
- Needs to communicate more effectively within the department.
- Needs to convey a more positive image of the company to customers and clients.
- Needs to convey the results of meetings to superiors with more clarity.
- Needs to demonstrate credibility and honesty in communication.
- Needs to improve ability to articulate positions and concepts.
- Needs to improve ability to communicate policies and procedures to others.
- Needs to improve ability to implement consensus decisions.
- Needs to improve ability to keep meetings on subject and on schedule.

- Needs to improve communications skills.
- Needs to improve management of teleconferences and conference calls.
- Needs to improve quality of written reports and memos.
- Needs to improve skills at facilitating meetings.
- Needs to improve skills at managing meetings.
- Needs to improve understanding of the corporate mission.
- Needs to improve vocabulary.
- Needs to incorporate the mission statement in important communications.
- Needs to learn to listen to suggestions and ideas of others.
- Needs to manage electronic messages better.
- Needs to respond more quickly to incoming communication.
- Needs to work on communicating management decisions with more skill.
- Needs to work to develop consensus-building strategies.
- Needs to work on expressing thoughts and instructions more clearly and concisely.
- Needs to work to avoid giving conflicting messages.
- Should be more diligent in documenting verbal communication when appropriate.
- Should communicate more effectively with other departments and divisions.
- Should devote more effort to managing electronic communications.
- Should encourage others to communicate effectively.
- Should find ways to improve communications with coworkers and supervisors.

- Should foster a more open and honest environment for the exchange of ideas.
- Should foster open communication among participants at meetings.
- Should improve ability to communicate the company's mission statement to customers and suppliers.
- Should improve ability to communicate with supervised staff.
- Should improve ability to help others communicate better.
- Should improve communications skills with customers and clients.
- Should improve foreign-language skills.
- Should improve management of foreign-language translation.
- Should improve understanding of proper committee procedure.
- Should improve use of communication technology.
- Should learn how to move undecided meeting participants to consensus.
- Should make more use of electronic communication services, including e-mail, groupware, and teleconferencing.
- Should work on ability to ask thoughtful and effective questions at meetings.
- Should work on new methods to manage teleconferences and conference calls.
- Should work to better apply the values of the corporate mission statement.
- Should work to improve ability to communicate well with superiors and supervisors.
- When speaking with coworkers does not always communicate clearly and directly.

Unsatisfactory

- Based on customer reports, has failed to convey a positive image of the company.
- Communicates with coworkers using language that is beyond their ability to clearly follow.
- Does not adequately inform superiors of results of meetings.
- Does not communicate effectively with other departments and divisions.
- Does not communicate well with coworkers and supervisors.
- Does not contribute thoughtful and effective questions at meetings.
- Does not encourage others to communicate openly and effectively.
- Does not express thoughts and instructions clearly and concisely.
- Does not follow through to implement consensus decisions.
- Does not foster an open and honest environment for the exchange of ideas.
- Failed to improve foreign-language skills to meet needs of the job.
- Fails to adequately document important verbal communication.
- Fails to manage electronic messages adequately.
- Fails to manage foreign-language translation tasks adequately.
- Fails to assist others to communicate ideas and proposals.
- Fails to communicate management decisions adequately.
- Fails to convey the company's mission statement to customers and suppliers.

- Fails to foster open communication among participants at meetings.
- Fails to listen to suggestions and ideas of others.
- Fails to make adequate use of electronic communication services, including e-mail, groupware, and teleconferencing.
- Fails to make use of available advanced communication technology.
- Fails to use proper committee procedure.
- Has demonstrated a lack of necessary communications skills and has failed to take steps to improve them.
- Has demonstrated a lack of understanding of and compliance with the corporate mission statement.
- Has failed to manage teleconferences and conference calls adequately.
- Has failed to oversee electronic communications policies adequately.
- Has failed to develop adequate consensus-building strategies.
- Has failed to establish effective communication within the department.
- Has failed to improve communications skills to meet needs of the job.
- Has failed to improve skills at facilitating meetings.
- Has failed to improve vocabulary to meet the needs of the job.
- Has failed to incorporate the mission statement in important communications.
- Has failed to take steps to improve ability to communicate with supervised staff.
- Has failed to take steps to improve skills at managing meetings.

- Has failed to work on new methods to manage teleconferences and conference calls.
- Is not able to convey a clear, straightforward message.
- Lacks personal credibility and honesty in communication.
- Quality of written reports and memos is not acceptable.
- Unable to communicate divisional and company goals adequately.
- Unable to communicate with customers and clients adequately.
- Unable to communicate with superiors and supervisors adequately.
- Unable to communicate effectively.
- Unable to communicate in a positive manner.
- Unable to keep meetings on subject and on schedule.
- Unable to move undecided meeting participants to consensus.
- Unable to properly communicate policies and procedures to others.
- Unable to respond to incoming communication in a timely manner.

Creativity

Key Verbs

creates	encourages	seeks
demonstrates	offers	shows
displays	promotes	

Key Nouns

alternatives	ingenuity	procedures
credit	insights	resourcefulness
ideas	issues	suggestions
independent thought	originality	

Meets or Exceeds

- Accepts new ideas from supervised staff, giving appropriate credit.
- Accepts suggestions for new procedures from supervisors.
- Consistently comes up with creative solutions.
- Consistently displays great originality in thought and deed.
- Consistently offers valuable insights into issues and problems.
- Constantly searching for new ideas and procedures.
- Contributes fresh ideas.
- Demonstrates great creativity in problem-solving.
- Does not let obstacles prevent completion of assignment; seeks appropriate alternative solutions.
- Does not rely only on tried-and-true solutions.
- Encourages coworkers to be inventive.
- Establishes an environment in which creativity flourishes.
- Has a great imagination and is able to channel that vision into workable solutions.
- Has proved to be a creative thinker and problem-solver.
- Helps redefine departmental policies when alternative solutions are found.
- Is always open to suggestions to improve operations.
- Is recognized as a creative thinker and problem-solver.

- Is recognized in the enterprise as someone who can promote creative thinking.
- Is willing to try alternative solutions.
- Plans ahead, considering alternative solutions to upcoming assignments.
- Promotes development of new ideas and solutions by others.
- Seeks alternative solutions.
- Seeks new procedures when appropriate, keeping within departmental guidelines.
- Seeks out new ideas from others.
- Shows a great deal of resourcefulness and ability to change directions when a better way is found.
- Shows great aptitude for appropriate experimentation.
- Shows great creativity in seeking solutions.
- Shows great ingenuity and resourcefulness.

Needs Improvement

- Has difficulty in changing the course of a project when another direction would be more appropriate.
- Lacks ingenuity and resourcefulness.
- Needs to demonstrate greater creativity in problem-solving.
- Needs to demonstrate more originality.
- Needs to find ways to get beyond unusual obstacles to completion of assignments.
- Should be more open to suggestions to improve operations.
- Should be willing to try alternative solutions.
- Should constantly search for new ideas and procedures.
- Should encourage new ideas from supervised staff, giving appropriate credit.

- Should make more effort to incorporate suggestions for new procedures by supervisors.
- Should plan ahead to consider alternative solutions to upcoming assignments.
- Should seek alternative solutions where necessary and appropriate.
- Should seek new procedures when appropriate, keeping within departmental guidelines.
- Should seek out new ideas from others.
- Should seek to contribute fresh ideas.
- Should seek to promote development of new ideas and solutions by others.
- Should work to establish an environment in which creativity flourishes.

Unsatisfactory

- Actively discourages independent thought.
- Actively discourages new solutions and procedures.
- Attempts solutions that violate departmental or enterprise policies.
- Discourages creativity.
- Discourages independent thought.
- Discourages new solutions and procedures.
- Establishes an environment that discourages independent thought and creativity.
- Fails to demonstrate creativity in problem-solving.
- Fails to follow departmental guidelines in seeking alternative solutions.
- Fails to give credit for new ideas and procedures suggested by others.

- Fails to originate any new ideas or to encourage others to do so.
- Fails to promote development of new ideas and solutions by others.
- Fails to seek out new ideas from others.
- Goes outside of departmental guidelines in search of alternative solutions.
- Has failed to demonstrate originality in performance of duties.
- Has proved to be inflexible or not open to imaginative ideas when they are different from the original plan.
- Has violated departmental or enterprise policies and guidelines with unauthorized procedures.
- Ignores new ideas suggested by supervised staff.
- Ignores new ideas suggested by supervisors.
- Is not open to new ideas and procedures.
- Is not open to suggestions to improve operations.
- Maintains an environment that discourages creativity and alternative solutions.
- Relies solely upon prescribed solutions; does not seek alternatives when necessary and appropriate.

Decision-Making Skills

Key Verbs

considers	demonstrates	seeks
consults	displays	shows
decides	expedites	

Key Nouns

alternatives	decisions	options
circumstances	forecasts	process
collaboration	guidelines	reasoning
computer models	innovation	risk
confidence	input	situations
creativity	judgment	
data	leader	

Meets or Exceeds

- A decisive leader.
- Able to expedite a decision when necessary.
- Able to make decisions in difficult or unusual situations.
- Able to make independent decisions, within guidelines.
- Able to make unpopular decisions when appropriate.
- Accepts a reasonable level of risk in decision-making, within departmental guidelines.
- Can be counted on to make excellent choices and informed decisions.
- Carefully considers facts and circumstances before making decisions.
- Carefully considers options in decision-making.
- Carefully considers the consequences and costs of decisions.
- Clearly communicates reasoning that underlies decisions.
- Communicates with others in a way that is reassuring and decisive.
- Considers a range of alternatives as part of decision-making process.

- Consults with supervisors and coworkers as necessary for major decisions.
- Decisions are well supported by accompanying data and reasoning.
- Displays sound judgment in decision-making.
- Does not make hasty decisions.
- Makes critical decisions with great confidence.
- Makes good use of computer models and decision-making tools.
- Makes well-considered decisions under pressure.
- Produces accurate and useful forecasts of the effect of decisions.
- Seeks collaborative input from colleagues on critical decisions where appropriate.
- Thinks outside the box; consistently comes up with innovative and creative decisions within guidelines.

Needs Improvement

- In certain situations, makes questionable choices.
- Lacks confidence in making critical decisions.
- Must carefully consider all options in decision-making.
- Must improve ability to make decisions in a timely fashion.
- Needs to avoid hasty, inadequately considered decisions.
- Needs to improve ability to make independent decisions, within guidelines.
- Needs to improve ability to consider facts and circumstances before making decisions.
- Needs to improve ability to make decisions in difficult or unusual situations.

- Needs to improve ability to make decisions under pressure.
- Needs to improvement judgment in decision-making.
- Needs to learn how to expedite a decision when necessary.
- Needs to learn to ask for guidance from coworkers and supervisors when appropriate.
- Needs to learn to forecast the effects of decisions with precision.
- Needs to learn to think outside the box, coming up with innovative and creative decisions within guidelines.
- Needs to consider the consequences and costs of decisions more carefully.
- Needs to communicate the reasoning that underlies decisions more clearly.
- Needs to provide better factual support for decisions.
- Should be willing to accept a reasonable level of risk in decision-making, within departmental guidelines.
- Should consider a range of alternatives as part of decision-making process.
- Should involve colleagues in critical decisions where appropriate.
- Should learn how to use computer models and decision-making tools in performance of job.
- Should work on ability to make unpopular decisions when appropriate.
- Should work on making communications and instructions more decisive.

Unsatisfactory

- Delivers communications and instructions to coworkers in a way that lacks decisiveness and confidence.

- Demonstrates poor judgment in decision-making.
- Displays poor decision-making skills under pressure.
- Does not handle pressure well.
- Does not make decisions in a timely fashion.
- Fails to consider facts and circumstances carefully before making decisions.
- Fails to communicate clearly the reasoning that underlies decisions.
- Fails to consider a range of alternatives as part of decision-making process.
- Fails to provide adequate supporting documents for decisions.
- Fails to seek input from colleagues where appropriate.
- Has failed to make use of available computer models and decision-making tools in performance of job.
- Has violated guidelines in decision-making.
- Ignores the consequences and costs of decisions.
- Is too rigid in decision-making.
- Is unwilling or unable to ask for guidance from coworkers and supervisors.
- Lacks confidence in making critical decisions.
- Makes hasty, inadequately considered decisions.
- Makes inaccurate forecasts of the effects of decisions.
- Makes risky decisions, outside of departmental guidelines.
- Makes uninspiring choices.
- Must carefully consider all options in decision-making.
- Needs to learn how to expedite a decision when necessary.
- Postpones decisions on difficult issues.
- Unable to make consistent, appropriate decisions in difficult or unusual situations.
- Unwilling to make unpopular decisions.

Dependability and Responsibility

Key Verbs

accepts	displays	meets
beats	exceeds	prepares
carries out	handles	seeks
demonstrates	manages	

Key Nouns

assignments	deadlines	reliable
challenges	dependable	responsible
commitment	guidelines	tasks
compliance	progress	values
conscientious	regulations	

Meets or Exceeds

- Is a conscientious and dependable worker.
- Is a highly dependable and responsible employee.
- Accepts responsibility for all assigned tasks, and those of supervised staff.
- Attendance record is commendable.
- Capable of bringing delayed or disrupted projects to conclusion.
- Committed to accomplishing all assignments on deadline.
- Communicates a steady presence.
- Consistently dependable in all assignments.
- Consistently meets or beats deadlines.
- Consistently meets or exceeds expectations on projects.
- Demonstrates solid values.

- Effectively carries out company guidelines as well as government regulations and accepts responsibility for compliance.
- Follows through on commitments.
- Handles high-stress assignments with great skill.
- Highly reliable and conscientious in every effort.
- Highly reliable attendance record.
- Inspires trust.
- Is a steady presence.
- Is recognized by coworkers for reliability.
- Keeps supervisors informed of the progress of assignments.
- Makes full use of available resources and facilities to accomplish assignments.
- Manages delegated responsibilities very well.
- Notably punctual.
- Prepares well for all assignments.
- Reliable, conscientious, and dependable.
- Seeks out new challenges and responsibilities.
- Very dependable in a crisis.
- Willing to accept responsibility for personal errors, or those by supervised staff.
- Willing to seek new assignments and responsibilities.
- Willingly accepts new responsibilities.

Needs Improvement

- Demonstrates wavering abilities.
- Needs to accept responsibility for all assigned tasks, and those of supervised staff.
- Needs to be better at meeting deadlines.
- Needs to be more dependable in completing assignments.

- Needs to be more punctual.
- Needs to be willing to accept responsibility for personal errors, or those by supervised staff.
- Needs to better carry out company guidelines as well as government regulations and accept responsibility for compliance.
- Needs to better demonstrate dependability and responsibility.
- Needs to improve ability to deal with high-stress assignments.
- Needs to improve ability to meet or beat deadlines.
- Needs to improve ability to perform in a crisis.
- Needs to improve attendance record.
- Needs to improve management of delegated responsibilities.
- Needs to keep supervisors better informed of the progress of assignments.
- Needs to work on projecting a more commanding and decisive presence.
- Should be more willing to accept new responsibilities.
- Should be more willing to seek new assignments and responsibilities.
- Should devote more effort to preparation for assignments.
- Should make better use of available resources and facilities to accomplish assignments.
- Should work to improve ability to meet or exceed expectations on projects.

Unsatisfactory

- Cannot be counted upon to follow through on commitments.
- Cannot be depended upon to complete assignments.

- Consistently misses deadlines.
- Delivers a poor attendance record.
- Delivers only the minimum effort.
- Denies responsibility for work.
- Does not accept responsibility for all assigned tasks, and those of supervised staff.
- Does not effectively carry out company guidelines or government regulations and accept responsibility for compliance.
- Does not handle high-stress assignments well.
- Does not prepare well for assignments.
- Does not regularly meet deadlines.
- Fails to adequately manage delegated responsibilities.
- Fails to keep supervisors adequately informed of the progress of assignments.
- Fails to reliably accomplish tasks or to inspire others to do so.
- Has an unreliable attendance record.
- Has demonstrated undependable and irresponsible actions.
- Has not demonstrated trustworthiness or loyalty.
- Refuses to accept responsibility for personal errors, or those by supervised staff.
- Regularly arrives late to work or meetings.
- Resists accepting new responsibilities.
- Seeks to avoid new responsibilities.
- Undependable and derelict in performance of duties.
- Undependable in a crisis.
- Unreliable and undependable in performance of duties.

Initiative in Accomplishing Goals

Key Verbs

anticipates	displays	seeks
demonstrates	manages	shows

Key Nouns

assignments	independence	solutions
deadlines	initiative	suggestions
flexibility	innovation	supervision
goals	procedures	tasks
ideas	responsibilities	

Meets or Exceeds

- Able to manage assignments and meet deadlines without supervision.
- Anticipates problems before they occur and seeks solutions.
- Consistently searches for better solutions.
- Contributes effective and practical suggestions.
- Demonstrates a go-to-it attitude.
- Demonstrates ability to accomplish assignments independently when appropriate.
- Demonstrates innovation and flexibility in solving problems.
- Eager to try new procedures and solutions.
- Is a real go-getter.
- Refuses to allow distractions to prevent timely completion of tasks.
- Reliably meets deadlines and inspires others to do the same by example.

- Requires little supervision.
- Seeks opportunities for new assignments and responsibilities.
- Shows ability to take the initiative in completing assignments and solving problems.
- Shows great initiative toward accomplishing goals.
- Willingly adapts procedures to incorporate new ideas.

Needs Improvement

- Is not forceful in initially tackling a problem.
- Needs to be able to manage assignments and meet deadlines without supervision.
- Needs to show ability to take the initiative in completing assignments and solving problems.
- Needs to show more initiative toward accomplishing goals.
- Needs to work to eliminate distractions in pursuit of goals.
- Should attempt to accomplish assignments independently when appropriate.
- Should be more willing to try new procedures and solutions.
- Should be willing to seek better solutions.
- Should demonstrate more innovation and flexibility in solving problems.
- Should require less supervision.
- Should seek opportunities for new assignments and responsibilities.
- Should show willingness to adapt procedures to incorporate new ideas.
- Should work to anticipate problems before they occur and seek solutions.

Unsatisfactory

- Does not anticipate problems before they occur and seek solutions.
- Does not demonstrate innovation or flexibility in solving problems.
- Fails to seek opportunities for new assignments and responsibilities.
- Fails to show initiative in accomplishing goals.
- Fails to take the initiative in completing assignments and solving problems.
- Is easily distracted and overwhelmed.
- Is too laid-back and reluctant to begin a project.
- Requires constant supervision.
- Resists adapting procedures to incorporate new ideas.
- Unable to accomplish assignments independently when appropriate.
- Unwilling to search for better solutions.
- Unwilling to try new procedures and solutions.

Judgment Skills

Key Verbs

considers	displays	shows
demonstrates	makes	

Key Nouns

actions	consequences	objectivity
alternate	deliberative	openness
conclusions	judgment	results

Meets or Exceeds

- Considers alternate conclusions and actions.
- Coworkers and supervisors respect and readily accept judgments.
- Decision-making process is consistently thoughtful and informed.
- Demonstrates openness and objectivity in making judgments.
- Is respected for the quality of judgments made.
- Is results-oriented.
- Makes judgments on the basis of careful and deliberative process.
- Shows excellent judgment.

Needs Improvement

- Does not keep in mind the consequences of actions.
- Must strive to become more fully informed when making decisions.
- Needs to consider alternate conclusions and actions.
- Needs to demonstrate more openness and objectivity in making judgments.
- Needs to use a more careful and deliberative process for judgments.

Unsatisfactory

- Displays closed mind in judgment process.
- Fails to consider alternate conclusions and actions.
- Has shown poor judgment in . . .
- Ignores possible consequences of bad choices.
- Is often reckless and uninformed when making decisions.

- Makes judgments without deliberation.
- Many judgments are questioned by coworkers and supervised staff.

Logic Skills

Key Verbs

considers	displays	thinks
demonstrates	shows	understands

Key Nouns

alternative	decisiveness	procedures
analysis	flexibility	process
common sense	logic	solutions
concepts	observation	theory
creativity	preparation	

Meets or Exceeds

- Considers alternative solutions.
- Demonstrates ability to prepare and analyze statistical data.
- Demonstrates careful deliberation in the decision-making process.
- Demonstrates understanding of complex job-related concepts and procedures.
- Displays flexibility and creativity in thinking.
- Displays good use of common sense.
- Displays sharp logic and decisiveness.
- Displays understanding of theoretical concepts related to job tasks.

- Displays understanding of theoretical concepts related to job tasks.
- Is a keen observer.
- Is an imaginative, creative thinker.
- Is an independent and creative thinker.
- Is willing to think outside the box in search of solutions.
- Makes consistently sound decisions.
- Makes good use of observations in decision-making process.
- Makes plans in anticipation of events.
- Relies on an excellent reservoir of common sense to make decisions.
- Shows exceptional logical skills.
- Thinks ahead.

Needs Improvement

- Is not consistent when making decisions.
- Needs to demonstrate better understanding of complex job-related concepts and procedures.
- Needs to demonstrate more flexibility and creativity in thinking.
- Needs to improve ability to observe events.
- Needs to improve ability to prepare and analyze statistical data.
- Needs to learn to make plans in anticipation of events.
- Needs to make better use of common sense in decision-making.
- Should be more deliberative in the decision-making process.
- Should improve capacity for creative thinking.

- Should improve use of observations in decision-making process.
- Should learn to consider alternative solutions.
- Should look for opportunities to think outside the box in search of solutions.
- Should strive to think ahead of day-to-day tasks.
- Should strive to improve understanding of theoretical concepts related to job tasks.
- Should work to improve understanding of theoretical concepts related to job tasks.
- Tends to overlook basic common sense when making decisions.

Unsatisfactory

- Is an indecisive manager.
- Does not demonstrate understanding of theoretical concepts related to job tasks.
- Does not display independent and creative thought.
- Does not show ability to learn from observation of events.
- Does not show evidence of advance planning.
- Fails to demonstrate understanding of theoretical concepts related to job tasks.
- Fails to make plans in anticipation of events.
- Fails to show flexibility and creativity in thinking.
- Has demonstrated inability to consider alternative solutions.
- Has not demonstrated an adequate level of common sense when making decisions.
- Has not demonstrated understanding of complex job-related concepts and procedures.

- Has not shown capacity for creative thinking.
- Has proved unable to accurately prepare and analyze statistical data.
- Is consistently on the wrong side of an issue.

Loyalty to the Organization

Key Verbs

demonstrates
displays
shows
supports

Key Nouns

allegiance	goals	respect
commitment	loyalty	steadfastness
dedication	positive attitude	

Meets or Exceeds

- Is a very dedicated and loyal worker.
- Can always be counted on for loyalty and dedication.
- Demonstrates steady loyalty to the enterprise and coworkers.
- Displays a commitment to the goals of the department and enterprise.
- Displays loyalty to supervisors and executives.
- Has developed strong loyalty from supervised staff.
- Has shown steadfast allegiance to the organization.
- Is consistent in support of the company.

- Respected for obvious dedication and loyalty.
- Supervised staff is fiercely loyal.
- Supports the enterprise through a positive attitude about policies and staff.

Needs Improvement

- Does not consistently show allegiance to the organization.
- Is not always consistent in support of the company.
- Needs to work to encourage loyalty from supervised staff.
- Should demonstrate support for the enterprise through a positive attitude about policies and staff.
- Should display a greater commitment to the goals of the department and enterprise.
- Should display more loyalty to supervisors and executives.
- Should strive to demonstrate loyalty to the enterprise and coworkers.
- Should work to better demonstrate dedication and loyalty to the enterprise.
- Should work to cultivate the loyalty of supervised staff.

Unsatisfactory

- Communicates a negative attitude and disloyalty to the enterprise.
- Demonstrates a lack of commitment to the goals of the department and enterprise.
- Demonstrates a lack of loyalty to supervisors and executives.
- Displays a negative attitude about policies and staff.
- Does not demonstrate dedication and loyalty to the enterprise.

- Does not show loyalty to the enterprise and coworkers.
- Fails to demonstrate support for the enterprise through a positive attitude about policies and staff.
- Fails to show loyalty to supervisors and executives.
- Has not shown commitment to the organization or coworkers.
- Shows no allegiance to the company.
- Supervised staff does not display loyalty.

Motivation to Accomplish Tasks and Goals

Key Verbs

demonstrates	inspires	shows
displays	motivates	

Key Nouns

ambition	effort	opportunity
attention	enthusiasm	results
commitment	goals	
driving force	motivation	

Meets or Exceeds

- Always gives full attention and effort to tasks.
- Is an energetic, goal-oriented employee.
- Is an enthusiastic and committed worker.
- Brings a high degree of enthusiasm to the job.
- Builds enthusiasm among supervised staff.
- Consistently finds ways to get past obstacles in way of goals.
- Consistently strives for excellence in all assignments.

- Consistently willing to take on new assignments.
- Demonstrates strong commitment to enterprise goals.
- Displays a results-oriented mindset.
- Displays appropriate ambition.
- Displays unsurpassed commitment to the goals of the enterprise.
- Gives the enterprise a competitive edge.
- Inspires others to strive toward higher goals.
- Is a goal-oriented worker.
- Is a highly motivated worker.
- Is able to inspire others to succeed.
- Is an ambitious and motivated employee.
- Is looked upon as a driving force within the organization.
- Is motivated by goals.
- Is strongly motivated to accomplish all assignments on time and to meet or exceed expectations.
- Learns from previous disappointments and failures.
- Makes the most of every opportunity.
- Motivates supervised staff to accomplish goals and increase productivity.
- Seeks extra work and assignments.
- Seeks out new assignments.
- Self-motivated to achieve the highest results.
- Willing to accept extra work assignments when necessary.

Needs Improvement

- Needs to show more evidence of motivation.
- Should attempt to bring more enthusiasm and commitment to the job.

- Should be more results-oriented.
- Should be more willing to accept extra work and assignments.
- Should be more willing to seek out new assignments.
- Should be more willing to take on new assignments.
- Should demonstrate a greater commitment to enterprise goals.
- Should demonstrate a willingness to accept extra work assignments when necessary.
- Should seek to demonstrate more ambition and motivation.
- Should seek to learn from previous disappointments and failures.
- Should strive for excellence in accomplishment of assignments.
- Should strive to find ways to get past obstacles to performance.
- Should strive to give full attention and effort to tasks.
- Should strive to improve motivation to accomplish all assignments on time and to meet or exceed expectations.
- Should strive to inspire others to do their best.
- Should strive to make the most of every opportunity.
- Should work to better motivate supervised staff to accomplish goals and increase productivity.
- Should work to build enthusiasm among supervised staff.
- Should work to inspire others to succeed.

Unsatisfactory

- Does little to motivate others to succeed.
- Does not demonstrate a commitment to enterprise goals.

- Does not demonstrate ambition or motivation to accomplish enterprise goals.
- Does not build enthusiasm among supervised staff.
- Does not give full attention and effort to tasks.
- Does not learn from previous disappointments and failures.
- Does not strive for excellence in accomplishment of assignments.
- Fails to encourage others to succeed.
- Fails to make the most of every opportunity.
- Fails to motivate supervised staff to better accomplish goals and increase productivity.
- Has not demonstrated a high degree of motivation to the job and organization.
- Repeats previous failures.
- Resists taking on new assignments.
- Shows little enthusiasm and commitment to the job.

Negotiating Skills

Key Verbs

    demonstrates
    displays
    negotiates
    shows

Key Nouns

conflicts	fairness	referee
deals	mediation	skills
disputes	mediator	tact
equitability	negotiations	training

Meets or Exceeds

- Demonstrates ability to end negotiations when an equitable deal is out of reach.
- Demonstrates ability to negotiate under pressure.
- Demonstrates ability to resolve conflicts fairly.
- Has sought special training as a negotiator.
- Is a proven and effective mediator.
- Is a skilled negotiator who represents the organization well.
- Is a strong and effective negotiator.
- Is able to get parties to reach a consensus that is perceived as balanced and fair.
- Is an established referee of disputes.
- Is capable of walking away from a bad deal.
- Negotiates with skill and tact.
- Recognized for fair and equitable negotiations.
- Shows ability to resolve conflicts.
- Works to prevent disputes before they happen.

Needs Improvement

- Needs to improve abilities as an effective negotiator.
- Needs to improve skills to be able to resolve conflicts fairly.
- Needs to learn to end negotiations when an equitable deal is out of reach.
- Needs to show better ability to negotiate under pressure.
- Needs to work on mediation skills.
- Often is heavy-handed when resolving conflicts.
- Should seek special training as a negotiator.
- Should strive to improve ability to conduct equitable negotiations.
- Should work to prevent disputes before they happen.

- Does not display tact in negotiations.
- Does not represent the organization well in negotiations.
- Has demonstrated a lack of skill as a negotiator.
- Has failed to seek special training as a negotiator.
- Has not demonstrated ability to resolve conflicts.
- Has not made efforts to prevent disputes before they happen.
- Has not performed well under pressure.
- Has not shown an ability to walk away from a bad deal.
- Has not successfully completed special training as a negotiator.
- Is not able to resolve conflicts.
- Is unable to referee or mediate a conflict.

Oral Presentation Skills

Key Verbs

communicates	displays	speaks
delivers	shows	

Key Nouns

clarity	grace	presentation
command	humor	remarks
contact	informality	speaker
enthusiasm	language	speech
formality	orator	

Meets or Exceeds

- Able to speak in informal situations without preparation.
- Is an accomplished public speaker.
- Communicates with clarity.
- Communicates well in all settings.
- Connects well with others.
- Delivers a message clearly and directly.
- Delivers public remarks clearly and confidently.
- Delivers remarks with humor and grace.
- Delivers speeches with enthusiasm.
- Has an excellent command of the language.
- Has sought special training in public speaking.
- Is a capable and effective speaker.
- Is an excellent communicator.
- Knows how to get an audience involved in a presentation.
- Makes a good impression in all verbal communications.
- Makes eye contact with an audience.
- Speaks clearly and directly.
- Understands what constitutes a good oral presentation.

Needs Improvement

- Has difficulty making a connection with audience.
- Needs more enthusiasm in speeches.
- Needs to become a more accomplished public speaker to meet job needs.
- Needs to improve ability to speak in informal situations without preparation.
- Needs to learn to connect with audience.
- Needs to learn to deliver a message clearly and directly.

- Needs to make eye contact with an audience.
- Should seek special training in public speaking.
- Should work to develop ability to deliver remarks with humor and grace.
- Should work to improve command of the language.

Unsatisfactory

- Demonstrates inability to connect with listeners.
- Does not connect well with audience.
- Does not speak clearly and directly.
- Has failed to take advantage of available training in public speaking.
- Has not demonstrated an ability to speak in informal situations without preparation.
- Has proved unable to establish a relationship with audience.
- Makes no eye contact in communication.

Persuasion Skills

Key Verbs

demonstrates	persuades	provides
displays	produces	uses
influences		

Key Nouns

ability	influence	reason
advocate	logic	reasonableness
credibility	objections	tact

Meets or Exceeds

- Demonstrates a proven ability to persuade.
- Demonstrates ability to gather support from supervised staff and superiors for positions.
- Demonstrates an ability to influence others in favor of a position.
- Displays logic and clarity in persuading others.
- Displays tact and reasonableness in dealing with others.
- Has the facility to sway others to accept a position.
- Is a convincing and believable advocate.
- Is a forceful and persuasive proponent of a position.
- Is adept at swaying others.
- Makes a credible case.
- Makes a winning argument.
- Produces reasonable and persuasive written communications.
- Provides excellent background materials for all positions and proposals.
- Uses logical arguments to effectively persuade others.
- Uses persuasive skills to overcome objections.

Needs Improvement

- Consistently unable to convince others of a point of view.
- Has difficulty in promoting a position.
- Is not a skillful advocate.
- Needs to develop skills to convince others to accept a position.
- Needs to improve ability to convince others.
- Needs to improve ability to persuade others.
- Needs to improve ability to produce reasonable and persuasive written communications.

- Needs to improve logic and clarity in efforts to persuade others.
- Should strive to provide better background materials for all positions and proposals.
- Should work to demonstrate tact and reasonableness in dealing with others.
- Should work to gather support from supervised staff and superiors for positions.
- Should work to improve persuasive skills to overcome objections.

Unsatisfactory

- Cannot advance a position.
- Does not produce reasonable and persuasive written communications.
- Fails to back up positions and proposals with adequate background materials.
- Has demonstrated inability to get points across.
- Has not demonstrated an ability to persuade others.
- Has not shown an ability to gather support from supervised staff and superiors for positions.
- Lacks tact in dealing with others.
- Lacks the ability to sway others.
- Makes unreasonable demands in dealing with others.
- Takes unreasonable positions in attempts at persuasion.

Presentation Skills

Key Verbs

appreciates	encourages	makes
delivers	helps	produces
demonstrates		

Key Nouns

answers	demonstrations	manner
appearance	energy	presentation
clarity	enthusiasm	questions
comments	graphics	understandability

Meets or Exceeds

- Appreciates the value of making a good appearance.
- Brings enthusiasm and energy to presentations.
- Delivers excellent oral presentations.
- Delivers information in clear and understandable manner.
- Delivers presentations clearly and with confidence.
- Demonstrates excellent use of technology to augment presentations.
- Encourages give-and-take with audience.
- Engages the audience in presentations.
- Gives informative and interesting demonstrations.
- Has sought specialized training in presentation skills.
- Helps train others in the effective use of computers and other tools for presentations.
- Is a skilled trainer on the use of computers and other tools for presentations.

- Makes excellent use of computer graphics, presentation programs, and other tools to improve presentations.
- Makes excellent use of graphs, art, animation, and other elements.
- Produces effective PowerPoint presentations.
- Seeks questions and comments from audience.
- Skillfully manages questions at presentations.
- Uses computer software to prepare compelling presentations.

Needs Improvement

- Must work to make demonstrations informative and interesting.
- Needs to dress in a more professional manner to command respect.
- Needs to improve ability to use computer software to prepare compelling presentations.
- Needs to improve oral presentation skills.
- Needs to make better use of technology to augment presentations.
- Needs to make excellent use of graphs, art, animation, and other elements.
- Should bring more enthusiasm and energy to presentations.
- Should encourage give-and-take with audience.
- Should improve skills at producing PowerPoint presentations.
- Should make better use of computer graphics, presentation programs, and other tools to improve presentations.
- Should make effort to train others in the effective use of computers and other tools for presentations.

- Should seek questions and comments from audience.
- Should seek specialized training in presentation skills.
- Should strive to better manage questions at presentations.
- Should strive to engage the audience in presentations.
- Should work to better deliver information in clear and understandable manner.

Unsatisfactory

- Displays lack of enthusiasm and energy for presentations.
- Does not deliver information in clear and concise manner.
- Does not make good use of computer graphics, presentation programs, and other tools to improve presentations.
- Does not manage questions at presentations well.
- Fails to demonstrate adequate oral presentation skills.
- Fails to encourage give-and-take with audience.
- Fails to make good use of computer software to prepare compelling presentations.
- Fails to make good use of technology to augment presentations.
- Fails to seek questions and comments from audience.
- Has failed to make good use of graphs, art, animation, and other elements.
- Has not made an effort to train others in the effective use of computers and other tools for presentations.
- Has not sought available specialized training in presentation skills.
- Has shown lack of capability to hold the attention of an audience.
- Lacks confidence in presentations.
- Makes a very poor personal appearance.

Problem-Solving Skills

Key Verbs

demonstrates
displays
solves

Key Nouns

alternatives	problems	technology
assignments	progress	tools
causes	responsibilities	troubleshooting
decisiveness	solutions	

Meets or Exceeds

- Is a decisive problem-solver.
- Capable of dealing with multiple problems at the same time.
- Capable of seeking and implementing standard and alternative solutions to problems.
- Demonstrates ability to determine the cause of problems.
- Demonstrates ability to prioritize and manage more than one problem at a time.
- Demonstrates skills at troubleshooting problems to determine solutions.
- Demonstrates strong skills in reasoning and analysis.
- Is capable of pinpointing potential trouble.
- Is not afraid to tackle a problem.
- Keeps supervisors informed of progress in solving problems, when appropriate.
- Makes excellent use of available technology and tools in

seeking and implementing solutions.
- Makes good use of proven problem-solving techniques when appropriate.
- Seeks alternate solutions when appropriate.
- Skilled in identifying and solving problems.
- Willing to accept new assignments and responsibilities in problem-solving.
- Works well with other individuals and departments in solving problems.

Needs Improvement

- Is sometimes intimidated in situations that present difficulties.
- Needs to become a more decisive problem-solver.
- Needs to better demonstrate ability to prioritize and manage more than one problem at a time.
- Needs to demonstrate improved skills in reasoning and analysis.
- Needs to develop skills necessary to pinpoint potential trouble.
- Needs to improve skills in identifying and solving problems.
- Needs to show ability to deal with multiple problems at the same time.
- Should be more willing to accept new assignments and responsibilities in problem-solving.
- Should keep supervisors better informed of progress in solving problems, when appropriate.
- Should make better use of available technology and tools in seeking and implementing solutions.
- Should make better use of proven problem-solving techniques when appropriate.
- Should make more effort to demonstrate ability to

troubleshoot problems to determine solutions.
- Should seek alternate solutions when appropriate.
- Should strive to better determine the cause of problems.
- Should strive to work better with other individuals and departments in solving problems.
- Should work to enhance ability to seek and implement standard and alternative solutions to problems.

Unsatisfactory

- Does not demonstrate adequate skills in reasoning and analysis.
- Does not make good use of available technology and tools in seeking and implementing solutions.
- Does not seek or employ alternate solutions when appropriate.
- Does not seek the cause of problems in developing solutions; deals only with the symptoms.
- Does not work well with other individuals and departments in solving problems.
- Fails to employ proven problem-solving techniques when appropriate.
- Fails to keep supervisors informed of progress in solving problems, when appropriate.
- Fails to pinpoint potential trouble spots.
- Has not demonstrated ability to deal with multiple problems at the same time.
- Has not shown capability of seeking and implementing standard and alternative solutions to problems.
- Has not shown facility to troubleshoot problems to determine solutions.

- Has not shown skill in identifying and solving problems.
- Has shown lack of ability to adequately respond to a crisis situation.
- Is unable to prioritize and manage more than one problem at a time.
- Takes an unreasonably long time before making decisions.
- Unwilling to accept new assignments and responsibilities in problem-solving.

Professionalism, Standards, and Ethics

Key Verbs

delivers	displays	produces
demonstrates	maintains	

Key Nouns

appropriateness	guidelines	professionalism
concepts	image	standards
cooperation	performance	trends
core principles	polish	values
ethics	principles	

Meets or Exceeds

- Consistently demonstrates professionalism in performance of job.
- Consistently dresses in an appropriate manner for the job.
- Continuously seeks to improve training and skills related to job.
- Delivers a professional image in all written communications within the organization and to clients.

- Demonstrates a commitment to a high level of professional ethics.
- Demonstrates a polished, professional manner on the telephone.
- Demonstrates commitment to performance of job in keeping with professional standards and ethics.
- Demonstrates understanding and commitment to core principles.
- Demonstrates years of professional experience in performance of job.
- Displays adherence to highest professional standards and ethics.
- Has contributed to the creation of a code of ethics for the organization.
- Is an officer of professional societies that set standards and ethics related to job.
- Is committed to assisting the entire organization establish and maintain the highest professional standards.
- Is recognized in the organization and among clients for possessing the highest ethical standards.
- Keeps current on trends and new concepts related to job.
- Led the way to establishment of a code of ethics.
- Maintains membership in highly regarded professional societies related to job.
- Makes full use of available technology and tools appropriate to the job.
- Presents the image of high moral values.
- Produces work of the highest professional quality.
- Takes full advantage of available training to advance career.

- Works well with individuals and other departments to enhance professionalism throughout the organization.
- Works well with outside consultants when appropriate.

Needs Improvement

- Does not demonstrate understanding of or commitment to core values.
- Needs to demonstrate a more polished and professional manner on the telephone.
- Needs to improve ability to work well with individuals and other departments to enhance professionalism throughout the organization.
- Needs to improve attention to appropriate dress for the job, as outlined in employee handbook.
- Needs to improve cooperation with outside consultants when appropriate.
- Needs to improve the quality of work produced.
- Needs to make better use of available technology and tools appropriate to the job.
- Needs to work on defining principles important to establishing goals.
- Should better demonstrate the benefit of years of experience in the field.
- Should consider membership in professional societies related to job.
- Should demonstrate commitment to a high level of professional ethics.
- Should keep more current on trends and new concepts related to job.
- Should seek to improve training and skills related to job.

- Should strive to demonstrate adherence to the highest professional standards and ethics.
- Should strive to help the organization create a code of ethics.
- Should strive to improve professional image in all written communications within the organization and to clients.
- Should take advantage of available training to advance career.
- Should work to assist the entire organization to establish and maintain the highest professional standards.

Unsatisfactory

- Displays commitment to values not in keeping with organizational goals or guidelines.
- Does not demonstrate ability to work well with outside consultants when appropriate.
- Does not demonstrate the benefit of years of experience in the field.
- Does not maintain membership in professional societies related to job.
- Does not make good use of available technology and tools appropriate to the job.
- Does not promote the importance of moral values by example.
- Does not take advantage of available training to advance career.
- Fails to consistently adhere to appropriate dress for the job, as outlined in employee handbook.
- Fails to consistently deliver a professional image in all written communications within the organization and to clients.

- Fails to demonstrate a commitment to a high level of professional ethics.
- Fails to demonstrate commitment to core values.
- Fails to display a polished and professional manner on the telephone.
- Fails to display adherence to highest professional standards and ethics.
- Fails to keep current on trends and new concepts related to the job.
- Fails to seek to improve training and skills related to job.
- Fails to work well with individuals and other departments to enhance professionalism throughout the organization.
- Has not shown commitment to assisting the entire organization establish and maintain the highest professional standards.
- Quality of work produced is below acceptable standards.

Quality of Work

Key Verbs

demonstrates
displays
produces
shows

Key Nouns

commitment
level
quality
superior

Meets or Exceeds

- Consistently produces work of exceptional quality.
- Displays commitment to quality at every level of the organization.
- Helps other individuals and departments achieve high levels of quality in their work.
- Is capable of a superior level of input.
- Is fully committed to the organization's mission statement on quality.
- Produces a superior product.
- Produces work of the highest quality.
- Shows dedication to producing work of the highest quality.
- Works well with individuals and other departments to promote high-quality work.

Needs Improvement

- Is inconsistent in level of work.
- Needs to display a commitment to the organization's mission statement on quality.
- Needs to improve overall quality of work.
- Needs to work to improve the level of work submitted.
- Should strive to produce work of the highest quality consistently.
- Should strive to demonstrate commitment to quality at every level of the organization.
- Should work to help other individuals and departments achieve high levels of quality in their work.

Unsatisfactory

- Does not deliver an acceptable level of quality as measured by standards.
- Does not work well with other individuals and departments to help them achieve high levels of quality in their assignments.
- Fails to demonstrate commitment to quality at every level of the organization.
- Fails to demonstrate commitment to the organization's mission statement on quality.
- Generally produces work of below-standard quality.
- Level of work is below par.

Sales Skills

Key Verbs

beats	delivers	helps
closes	demonstrates	provides
converts	displays	represents

Key Nouns

commitment	deals	respect
competitive analysis	leads	sales
customer loyalty	performance	sales pitch
customer service	politeness	strategies

Meets or Exceeds

- Always available to customers to answer questions and assist in solving problems.
- Brings in a high number of new customers.
- Closes a high percentage of deals.
- Consistently beats sales targets.
- Consistently delivers sales performance that meets or exceeds goals.
- Converts a high percentage of leads to sales.
- Conveys customer wishes for new features to marketing and design departments.
- Delivers a sales pitch that is both articulate and informative.
- Delivers a winning pitch.
- Demonstrates a commitment to building and maintaining customer loyalty.
- Demonstrates a high degree of ethics in sales.
- Demonstrates an ability to close deals.
- Demonstrates excellent ability to assist customers in resolving problems with products.
- Demonstrates excellent results in generating new sales leads.
- Demonstrates excellent sales performance.
- Demonstrates good use of competitive analysis in setting sales strategies.
- Demonstrates strong abilities in training sales staff.
- Develops a large number of new sales leads.
- Displays broad knowledge and understanding of the product line.
- Displays excellent sales research skills.
- Does not concentrate only on price; sells product on the basis of features, service, and support.

- Handles unreasonable customers politely and professionally.
- Helps customers receive excellent service and support.
- Helps customers resolve complaints and problems.
- Is a leading salesperson.
- Is a top salesperson.
- Is an excellent candidate for a sales management position.
- Is polite and professional in dealing with customer complaints.
- Is well respected by customers for knowledge of the industry.
- Keeps current on new developments in the industry and adjusts sales strategies and techniques accordingly.
- Keeps in regular touch with customers.
- Leads the department in sales.
- Makes excellent use of available technology and tools to generate leads and make sales.
- Makes good use of marketing materials including advertising and promotional efforts.
- Provides excellent customer service.
- Receives highest grades from customers for quality of sales and service.
- Represents the company very well in sales presentations.
- Retains a high percentage of existing customers.
- Scores in highest category for customer satisfaction in surveys.
- Seeks and completes sales training courses to improve job performance.
- Willing to assist other salespeople and departments in sales campaigns.
- Works well with other individuals and departments in team sales efforts.
- Works with established customers to ensure excellent service.

Needs Improvement

- Does not consistently meet or beat sales targets.
- Must be more polite and professional in dealing with customer complaints.
- Must become more resourceful in making a sales pitch.
- Must work to be more coherent in articulation of products and services.
- Needs to better assist customers in resolving complaints and problems.
- Needs to better demonstrate a commitment to building and maintaining customer loyalty.
- Needs to better display a broad knowledge and understanding of the product line.
- Needs to demonstrate to customers a better knowledge of the industry.
- Needs to improve ability to train sales staff.
- Needs to improve customer satisfaction scores in surveys.
- Needs to keep current on new developments in the industry and adjust sales strategies and techniques accordingly.
- Needs to learn better skills to handle unreasonable customers politely and professionally.
- Needs to make better use of marketing materials including advertising and promotional efforts.
- Needs to move beyond a concentration only on price, selling product on the basis of features, service, and support.
- Needs to provide better customer service.
- Should be more available to customers to answer questions and assist in solving problems.
- Should be more regularly in touch with customers.

- Should be more willing to assist other salespeople and departments in sales campaigns.
- Should better convey customer wishes for new features to marketing and design departments.
- Should better demonstrate a high degree of ethics in sales.
- Should improve sales research skills.
- Should increase efforts to work with established customers to ensure excellent service.
- Should make better use of available technology and tools to generate leads and make sales.
- Should make better use of competitive analysis in setting sales strategies.
- Should make efforts to assist customers to receive excellent service and support.
- Should seek and complete sales training courses to improve job performance.
- Should seek to better cooperate with other individuals and departments in team sales efforts.
- Should seek to convert a higher percentage of leads to sales.
- Should seek to improve skills to be able to improve ability to close deals.
- Should strive to bring in more new customers.
- Should strive to generate new sales leads.
- Should strive to improve skills in sales management for career advancement.
- Should strive to retain a higher percentage of existing customers.
- Should work to assist customers in resolving problems with products.

Unsatisfactory

- According to customers, does not demonstrate a good knowledge of the industry.
- According to customers, does not provide a high level of customer service.
- Closes deals at a below-average rate.
- Consistently falls short of sales targets.
- Converts a below-average percentage of leads to sales.
- Delivery is flat and uninspiring.
- Demonstrates lack of willingness to assist other salespeople and departments in sales campaigns.
- Does not consistently convey customer wishes for new features to marketing and design departments.
- Does not consistently represent the company well in sales presentations.
- Does not keep in regular touch with customers.
- Does not make good use of competitive analysis in setting sales strategies.
- Does not make good use of marketing materials including advertising and promotional efforts.
- Does not offer assistance to customers in resolving complaints and problems.
- Does not produce effective sales research.
- Does not receive high scores for customer satisfaction in surveys.
- Fails to demonstrate a commitment to building and maintaining customer loyalty.
- Fails to demonstrate a high degree of ethics in sales.
- Fails to display a broad knowledge and understanding of the product line.

- Fails to handle unreasonable customers politely and professionally.
- Fails to keep current on new developments in the industry and adjusts sales strategies and techniques accordingly.
- Fails to make good use of available technology and tools to generate leads and make sales.
- Fails to make sales presentations that move beyond price, selling product on the basis of features, service, and support.
- Fails to seek and complete sales training courses to improve job performance.
- Has demonstrated substandard sales performance.
- Has not demonstrated ability to cooperate with other individuals and departments in team sales efforts.
- Has not generated a sufficient number of sales leads.
- Has not made efforts to assist customers to receive excellent service and support.
- Has not made efforts to work with established customers to ensure excellent service.
- Has not shown ability to adequately train sales staff.
- Has not shown commitment to assist customers in resolving problems with products.
- Has not shown success in bringing in new customers.
- Has shown lack of availability to customers to answer questions and assist in solving problems.
- Is not always polite and professional in dealing with customer complaints.
- Retains a below-average percentage of existing customers.

Secretarial and Clerical Skills

Key Verbs

adapts	displays	presents
demonstrates	handles	represents

Key Nouns

dependability	policies	punctuality
organization	polish	refinement
planning		

Meets or Exceeds

- Adapts well to changes in policies and job demands.
- Can be counted on as a highly dependable member of staff.
- Consistently displays a high degree of organization and planning.
- Demonstrates great attention to detail and accuracy.
- Displays ability to cooperate with other individuals and departments.
- Handles suggestions and criticisms well.
- Is professional in dealing with staff and public.
- Is always punctual, with an excellent attendance record.
- Presents a polished and refined image.
- Represents the company well.

Needs Improvement

- Has an acceptable attendance record.
- Is generally able to adapt to changes in policies and the demands of the job.

- Is generally dependable.
- Is generally well organized, but could improve methods.
- Is usually cooperative with others.
- Needs to better represent the company in actions and words.
- Needs to work on presenting a more professional image.
- Produces work at a reasonable level of detail and accuracy, with room for improvement.
- Usually handles suggestions and criticisms well.

Unsatisfactory

- Cannot be depended upon for critical and time-sensitive tasks.
- Does not handle suggestions and criticisms well.
- Does not readily adapt to changes in policies and the demands of the job.
- Has a poor or unacceptable attendance record.
- Is not a good representative for the company.
- Is often unwilling to cooperate with others.
- Is poorly organized.
- Presents an image not appropriate for professional level.
- Work does not meet acceptable standards for level of detail and accuracy.

Self-Improvement and Learning Skills

Key Verbs

demonstrates
develops
displays
seeks

Key Nouns

advancement	expert	self-motivation
ambition	goals	seminars
background	market strategies	skills
career goals	resource	training
courses		

Meets or Exceeds

- Adapts quickly to changes in the market or enterprise strategics.
- Can be counted on to contribute to improvement in the organization.
- Career goals are clearly identified.
- Committed to improving job performance.
- Continually improves job skills.
- Continuously seeks to enhance skills and background.
- Contributes worthy ideas to improve individual and enterprise performance.
- Demonstrates ambition for advancement.
- Displays commitment to improving job-related expertise.
- Encourages suggestions for improvement from coworkers.
- Establishes an environment conducive to learning.
- Is always eager to learn new skills and background.
- Is an expert in the field.
- Is open to innovative and fresh proposals.
- Is recognized in the company as an expert and an important resource.
- Keeps up-to-date on changing job requirements.
- Learns new methods quickly and easily.

- Makes quick adjustment to new policies and procedures.
- Pursues advanced education in the field.
- Seeks every opportunity to improve professional skills and background.
- Seeks unique and innovative ways to improve performance.
- Seeks ways to assist supervised staff in focusing on weaknesses to improve performance.
- Self-motivated to improve job skills and performance.
- Sets reasonable goals for boosting performance.
- Takes every opportunity to attend seminars and courses to keep up-to-date.
- Welcomes new ideas and procedures.
- Welcomes growth in personal development.

Needs Improvement

- Needs to adjust more quickly to new policies and procedures.
- Needs to become self-motivated to improve job skills and performance.
- Needs to demonstrate receptiveness to new ideas and procedures.
- Needs to keep up-to-date on changing job requirements.
- Needs to learn to adapt more quickly to changes in the market or enterprise strategies.
- Needs to more clearly identify career goals.
- Needs to work on encouraging input from coworkers on ideas for improvement.
- Should continuously seek to enhance skills and background.

- Should demonstrate more interest in learning new skills and background.
- Should pursue advanced education in the field.
- Should seek to contribute worthy ideas to improve individual and enterprise performance.
- Should seek ways to assist supervised staff in focusing on weaknesses to improve performance.
- Should set reasonable goals to boost performance.
- Should take every opportunity to attend seminars and courses to keep up-to-date.
- Should take more advantage of training opportunities to improve professional skills and background.
- Should work on improving job-related expertise.
- Should work to advance personal growth and development.
- Should work to establish an environment conducive to learning.
- Should work to gain recognition in the company as an expert and an important resource.
- Should work to improve job performance.

Unsatisfactory

- Demonstrates lack of interest in learning new skills and background.
- Does not adjust quickly to new policies and procedures.
- Does not contribute worthy ideas to improve individual and enterprise performance.
- Does not create an environment conducive to learning.
- Does not keep up-to-date on changing job requirements.
- Does not learn new methods easily or quickly.

- Does not pursue advanced education in the field.
- Does not take advantage of seminars and courses to keep up-to-date.
- Fails to adapt quickly to changes in the market or enterprise strategies.
- Fails to assist supervised staff in focusing on weaknesses to improve performance.
- Fails to continuously enhance skills and background.
- Fails to keep current on professional skills.
- Fails to take advantage of available training to improve professional skills and background.
- Fails to work to gain recognition in the company as an expert and an important resource.
- Has not set reasonable goals to boost performance.
- Has not worked to improve job performance.
- Is close-minded about accepting input from coworkers.
- Lacks self-motivation to improve job skills and performance.
- Resists new ideas and procedures.
- Shows no desire to enhance personal growth and development.
- Shows no inclination to improve job-related expertise.

Writing Skills

Key Verbs

conveys	demonstrates	produces
delivers	prepares	responds

Key Nouns

computer tools	impression	positivity
effectiveness	letters	proposals
e-mail	memos	tools
grammar	mission statement	vocabulary
image		

Meets or Exceeds

- Conveys a positive impression in written communication.
- Creates substantial and meaningful reports.
- Delivers a positive image of the organization in written communication to clients and customers.
- Delivers written communication that conveys the mission statement.
- Demonstrates ability to produce effective written communication that yields results.
- Demonstrates skills as an editor of written communication by others.
- Displays considerable knowledge of the industry in written communication.
- Is an excellent communicator.
- Makes excellent use of computer tools to check spelling and grammar.
- Makes excellent use of e-mail to communicate with supervised staff and superiors.
- Possesses excellent vocabulary and grammatical skills.
- Prepares clear, concise written communications.
- Produces clear and concise manuals and guidelines.
- Produces effective proposals that gain management approval.

- Produces written communication free of errors in spelling, grammar, and formatting.
- Quality of written communication is outstanding.
- Responds to memos and letters quickly and professionally.

Needs Improvement

- Must improve ability to produce effective proposals that gain management approval.
- Must respond to memos and letters quicker, and in a professional manner.
- Needs to be aware that all communication should not be answered in the same style.
- Needs to create substantial and meaningful reports.
- Needs to deliver written communication that conveys the mission statement.
- Needs to improve ability to deliver a positive image of the organization in written communication to clients and customers.
- Needs to improve ability to produce clear, concise written communications.
- Needs to improve ability to produce effective written communications that yield results.
- Needs to improve knowledge of the industry and demonstrate this in written communication.
- Needs to improve quality of written communication.
- Needs to improve skills as an editor of written communication by others.
- Needs to improve use of e-mail to communicate with supervised staff and superiors.
- Needs to improve vocabulary and grammatical skills.

- Needs to learn to convey a positive impression in written communication.
- Needs to make better use of computer tools to check spelling and grammar.
- Needs to produce clear and concise manuals and guidelines.
- Needs to work to produce written communication free of errors in spelling, grammar, and formatting.
- Should develop differing styles for formal correspondence and other communications.

Unsatisfactory

- Does not convey a positive impression in written communication.
- Does not demonstrate acceptable vocabulary and grammatical skills.
- Does not demonstrate knowledge of the industry in written communication.
- Does not produce an acceptable level of written work.
- Does not properly use e-mail to communicate with supervised staff and superiors.
- Fails to convey the mission statement in written communication.
- Fails to deliver a positive image of the organization in written communication to clients and customers.
- Fails to make use of available computer tools to check spelling and grammar.
- Fails to produce substantial and meaningful reports.
- Fails to quickly and professionally respond to memos and letters.

- Fails to show abilities as an editor of written communication by others.
- Has displayed an inability to produce clear, concise written communications.
- Has failed to demonstrate ability to produce effective written communications that yield results.
- Has not demonstrated ability to produce clear and concise manuals and guidelines.
- Produces ineffective and unrealistic proposals that fail to gain management approval.
- Written communication includes errors in spelling, grammar, and formatting.
- Written communication is incoherent.

Chapter 6

QUANTITATIVE ATTRIBUTES

WHEN WE CONSIDER THE QUANTITATIVE ATTRIBUTES of an employee, we are looking at characteristics that can be measured against some sort of objective rule or counter. We can reasonably expect a clerical employee to consistently demonstrate mastery of a computer application, ask a manager to accurately forecast consumption or production or sales, or insist that every staffer arrive for work on time.

- Accomplishment of tasks and goals
- Accuracy and precision
- Computer skills
- Cost and resources management
- Knowledge of job and industry
- Planning and scheduling skills
- Setting goals and objectives
- Technical competence
- Time management and prioritization
- Work habits, punctuality, and attendance

Accomplishment of Tasks and Goals

Key Verbs

accomplishes	completes	meets and exceeds
achieves	delivers	produces

Key Nouns

achievements	deadlines	managerial skills
change	goals	progress
consistency		

Meets or Exceeds

- Accomplishes above-average achievements.
- Accomplishes long-term or permanent change.
- Achieves significant accomplishments.
- Brings excellent managerial skills to the table.
- Can be depended upon to meet or beat deadlines.
- Completes assignments in a timely and satisfactory manner.
- Consistently contributes to bottom-line results
- Consistently delivers outstanding results.
- Consistently meets or beats deadlines.
- Consistently meets or exceeds organizational goals.
- Delivers consistent performance.
- Delivers highest levels of performance and work product.
- Demonstrates ability to determine the multiple tasks involved in a project and prioritize their completion.
- Helps supervised staff to establish plans to accomplish goals.
- Is goal-oriented.

- Keeps management appropriately informed of progress toward meeting deadlines.
- Meets and exceeds personal or professional goals.
- Recognized in the company for achievements.
- Sets reasonable and appropriate goals for supervised coworkers.

Needs Improvement

- Must improve ability to determine the multiple tasks involved in a project and prioritize their completion.
- Must keep management appropriately informed of progress toward meeting deadlines.
- Must learn to set reasonable and appropriate goals for supervised coworkers.
- Must work to consistently meet or exceed organizational goals.
- Needs to be improve ability to complete tasks in a timely manner.
- Needs to be more goal-oriented.
- Needs to contribute consistently to bottom-line results.
- Needs to effect long-term or permanent change.
- Needs to help supervised staff to establish plans to accomplish goals.
- Needs to improve consistency of performance.
- Needs to improve level of achievement.
- Needs to improve quality of performance and work product.
- Needs to meet and exceed personal or professional goals.
- Needs to raise profile in the company for achievements.

- Needs to work to improve administrative skills.
- Should aim for above-average achievements.
- Should strive to meet or beat deadlines consistently.
- Should work to demonstrate capability to be depended upon to meet or beat deadlines.

Unsatisfactory

- Cannot be depended upon to meet or beat deadlines.
- Consistently goes past deadlines for completion of assignments.
- Delivers below-average achievements.
- Does not help supervised staff to establish plans to accomplish goals.
- Does not keep management appropriately informed of progress toward meeting deadlines.
- Does not meet or exceed personal or professional goals.
- Does not set reasonable and appropriate goals for supervised coworkers.
- Fails to concentrate on goals.
- Fails to contribute to bottom-line results consistently.
- Fails to meet or exceed organizational goals consistently.
- Fails to deliver consistent performance.
- Fails to deliver significant contributions to the company.
- Has not demonstrated ability to determine the multiple tasks involved in a project and prioritize their completion.
- Has not made any notable achievements in the company.
- Is ineffective as an administrator or manager.
- Regularly fails to complete tasks on time.
- Unable to deliver acceptable levels of performance and work product.

Accuracy and Precision

Key Verbs

achieves	excels at	recognizes
conforms to	maintains	strives for
delivers		

Key Nouns

accuracy	results	tolerances
forecasts	specifications	tools
records	standards	

Meets or Exceeds

- Achieves a high degree of accuracy.
- Conforms to expected tolerances.
- Delivers accurate and precise results.
- Delivers highly accurate forecasts.
- Delivers work of the highest accuracy and precision.
- Delivers work that meets or exceeds specifications.
- Documents work well.
- Gets to the truth.
- Is scrupulous in pursuit of accuracy.
- Maintains accurate records.
- Maintains meticulous attention to detail.
- Maintains meticulous records on projects.
- Meets or exceeds standards.
- Recognizes the need for a high degree of accuracy.
- Seeks perfection in every assignment.
- Seeks to use recognized tools for all forecasts.

- Strives for accuracy in all forecasts.
- Strives for perfection.
- Strives to avoid errors at every step.

Needs Improvement

- Must better document work.
- Must conform to expected tolerances.
- Must deliver accurate forecasts.
- Must maintain accurate records.
- Needs to achieve a higher degree of accuracy.
- Needs to deliver accurate and precise results.
- Needs to deliver work of higher accuracy and precision.
- Needs to deliver work that meets or exceeds specifications.
- Needs to devote greater attention to detail.
- Needs to improve quality of work to meet or exceed standards.
- Needs to maintain better records on projects.
- Needs to recognize the need for a high degree of accuracy.
- Needs to strive for greater accuracy in forecasts.
- Needs to strive for perfection.
- Needs to strive to avoid errors at every step.
- Needs to take more care in pursuit of accuracy.
- Needs to use recognized tools for all forecasts.
- Should strive for perfection on every assignment.

Unsatisfactory

- Fails to deliver work that meets or exceeds specifications.
- Fails to maintain acceptable records on projects.
- Fails to maintain accurate records.
- Fails to recognize the need for accuracy.

- Fails to work to avoid errors.
- Is ineffective in maintaining attention to detail.
- Refuses to use recognized tools for forecasting.
- Unable to achieve an acceptable degree of accuracy.
- Unable to conform to expected tolerances.
- Unable to deliver accurate and precise results.
- Unable to deliver accurate forecasts.
- Unable to deliver work of acceptable accuracy and precision.
- Unable to deliver work products without errors.
- Unable to meet standards.
- Unwilling to document work.
- Work is careless and sloppy.

Computer Skills

Key Verbs

assists	displays	promotes
demonstrates	possesses	

Key Nouns

applications	online	support
e-mail	productivity	training
expert	resource	troubleshooting
fundamentals		

Meets or Exceeds

- Ably designed a departmental computer support operation.
- Attends appropriate trade shows, seminars, and demonstrations to learn about new technologies.

- Demonstrates strong understanding of computers.
- Demonstrates excellent skills in computer troubleshooting.
- Developed and oversees an excellent program to train employees on computer tasks.
- Has ably managed training of new employees on computer tasks.
- Has established appropriate guidelines governing the proper use of online resources.
- Has helped establish important guidelines on the proper use of the Internet and e-mail by employees.
- Has helped the organization improve productivity through the use of computers.
- Is a "geek" in the very best sense.
- Is a strong proponent of the use of computers in the enterprise.
- Is a valuable source of information on computer usage and hardware for coworkers.
- Is an acknowledged expert on the application of computer software to our needs.
- Keeps current on new computer hardware and software.
- Keeps current on new technologies and applications.
- Possesses a strong base of knowledge on computer fundamentals.
- Promotes the benefits of computers throughout the enterprise.
- Promotes the effective use of online resources.
- Promotes the use of the computer to automate common office tasks.
- Recognized as a reliable and effective troubleshooter.
- Recognized as an essential in-house expert on computer problems.
- Recognized as an in-house computer expert.

Needs Improvement

- Fails to keep current on changes in the industry.
- Needs to develop a computer training program for new employees.
- Needs to develop an effective program to train employees on computer tasks.
- Needs to establish appropriate guidelines to govern the proper use of online resources.
- Needs to help establish guidelines on the proper use of the Internet and e-mail by employees.
- Needs to implement a departmental computer support operation.
- Needs to improve computer knowledge.
- Needs to improve skills in computer troubleshooting.
- Needs to improve understanding of computer fundamentals.
- Should attend appropriate trade shows, seminars, and demonstrations to learn about new technologies.
- Should become a more forceful proponent of the use of computers in the enterprise.
- Should devote time to keeping current on new technologies and applications.
- Should improve standing as an expert on the application of computer software to our needs.
- Should keep current on new computer hardware and software.
- Should promote the benefits of computers throughout the enterprise.
- Should promote the effective use of online resources.
- Should promote the use of the computer to automate common office tasks.

- Should seek new ways to improve productivity through the use of computers.
- Should strive to become a source of information and assistance to others.

Unsatisfactory

- Fails to adequately use computer tools and hardware specified in job description.
- Has failed to assist others in the use of computers, as asked in job description.
- Has failed to become proficient in necessary computer skills.
- Has failed to develop a computer training program for new employees.
- Has failed to develop an effective program to train employees on computer tasks.
- Has failed to enhance skills as a computer troubleshooter.
- Has failed to establish effective guidelines on the proper use of the Internet and e-mail.
- Has failed to keep current on new computer hardware and software.
- Has failed to keep current on new technologies and applications.
- Has failed to seek ways to improve productivity through the use of computers.
- Has ignored requests to establish guidelines on the proper use of the Internet and e-mail by employees.
- Has ignored the need for a departmental computer support operation.
- Has ignored the need to establish appropriate guidelines to govern the proper use of online resources.

- Has not attended appropriate trade shows, seminars, and demonstrations to learn about new technologies.
- Has not contributed to the migration of common office tasks to the computer.
- Has not demonstrated expertise in the application of computer software to our needs.
- Has not promoted the effective use of online resources.
- Has not sought to promote the use of computers in the enterprise.
- Has proved unable to demonstrate grasp of even the most fundamental computer skills.
- Lacks basic understanding of computer fundamentals.

Cost and Resources Management

Key Verbs and Adverbs

controls	makes	monitors
effectively	manages	oversees
keeps		

Key Nouns

accounting	cost accounting	goals
audits	cost of manufacture	information
bottom line	cost of services	negotiation
budget objectives	costs	reduction
budgets	expenses	renegotiation
constraints	finances	variances
controls		

Meets or Exceeds

- Analyzes financial information with great skill.
- Applies standard accounting principles to development and management of budgets.
- Carefully monitors cost accounting.
- Consistently meets or stays below budgetary goals.
- Constructs realistic and workable budgets.
- Consults with management, when appropriate, about budget variances.
- Creates realistic budget objectives.
- Demands justification for increases in cost.
- Demonstrates good understanding of standard accounting principles.
- Demonstrates remarkable accuracy in estimating costs.
- Develops realistic and efficient budgets.
- Develops reasonable budgets.
- Effectively controls costs.
- Effectively manages variances from budget.
- Encourages others to work within budgetary limits.
- Establishes and maintains appropriate audit systems.
- Establishes enterprisewide strategies to reduce travel and entertainment costs.
- Establishes realistic goals for cost of manufacture.
- Establishes realistic goals for cost of services.
- Finds ways to reduce costs without compromising quality.
- Follows recognized principles of fiscal auditing.
- Has developed plans that have saved the company (thousands/millions) of dollars.
- Has negotiated new contracts that have reduced costs.
- Is fiscally savvy and bottom-line oriented.

- Keeps a close eye on the use of company resources.
- Keeps a close eye on variable costs.
- Keeps the bottom line in mind.
- Keeps within or below the allotted budget.
- Maintains a close eye on the cost of management decisions.
- Maintains strict controls on expense accounts, including close monitoring of invoices and receipts.
- Maintains strong and effective cost controls.
- Makes good use of company resources.
- Makes operational decisions based on budgetary constraints.
- Makes sound, well-considered financial decisions.
- Makes the most of available funds and resources.
- Manages resources and staff well.
- Manages the budget effectively.
- Monitors travel and entertainment expenses closely.
- Oversees inventory levels properly to control costs.
- Oversees programs to reduce manufacturing waste.
- Oversees programs to reduce office supply waste.
- Presents rational and balanced financial plans.
- Seeks new suppliers and contractors to reduce costs when appropriate.
- Seeks new targets for cost reduction.
- Seeks to renegotiate contracts to reduce costs when appropriate.
- Seeks ways to control and reduce travel and entertainment expenses.
- Shows deep understanding of principles of cost accounting.
- Stays within budgetary constraints.

- Strives to find hidden costs.
- Strives to improve cost-profit ratios where possible.
- Works with human resources to reduce costs through proper scheduling of work force.
- Works with others to establish and maintain enterprisewide cost controls.
- Works within the budget.

Needs Improvement

- Could make better use of company resources.
- Is not even-handed when proposing financial plans.
- Needs to be able to provide information on the cost of management decisions.
- Needs to be more creative and forceful in price negotiations with suppliers.
- Needs to better manage variances from budget.
- Needs to consult with management, when appropriate, about budget variances.
- Needs to create more realistic budget objectives.
- Needs to demonstrate ability to properly analyze financial information.
- Needs to develop reasonable budgets.
- Needs to devote more attention to monitoring inventory levels to control costs.
- Needs to improve ability to meet or stay below budgetary goals.
- Needs to improve ability to construct realistic and workable budgets.
- Needs to improve ability to effectively manage a budget.
- Needs to improve ability to establish realistic goals for the cost of manufacture.

- Needs to improve ability to establish realistic goals for the cost of services.
- Needs to improve ability to make sound financial decisions.
- Needs to improve ability to manage resources and staff.
- Needs to improve ability to stay within budgetary constraints.
- Needs to improve accuracy in estimating costs.
- Needs to improve skills at developing realistic and efficient budgets.
- Needs to improve understanding of standard accounting principles.
- Needs to keep a closer eye on the bottom line.
- Needs to keep within or below the allotted budget.
- Needs to learn to apply standard accounting principles to development and management of budgets.
- Needs to learn to make the most of available funds and resources.
- Needs to keep an eye on opportunities for cost savings and demonstrate the necessary flexibility to take advantage of them.
- Needs to seek ways to improve cost-profit ratios.
- Needs to show deeper understanding of principles of cost accounting.
- Needs to work within the established budget.
- Should improve ability to carefully monitor cost accounting.
- Should improve ability to use recognized principles of fiscal auditing.
- Should improve capabilities to effectively control costs.

- Should improve capabilities to maintain strong and effective cost controls.
- Should maintain stricter controls on expense accounts, including close monitoring of invoices and receipts.
- Should monitor travel and entertainment expenses more closely, in keeping with policy.
- Should more closely monitor variable costs.
- Should seek new targets for cost reduction.
- Should seek enterprisewide strategies to reduce travel and entertainment costs.
- Should seek new suppliers and contractors to reduce cost when appropriate.
- Should seek to reduce manufacturing waste.
- Should seek to reduce office supply waste.
- Should seek to renegotiate contracts to reduce costs when appropriate.
- Should seek ways to control and reduce travel and entertainment expenses.
- Should seek ways to reduce costs without compromising quality.
- Should show better understanding of bottom line costs.
- Should strive to find hidden costs.
- Should strive to improve operational decisions in light of budgetary constraints.
- Should work to establish and maintain appropriate audit systems.
- Should work with human resources to reduce costs through proper scheduling of work force.
- Should work with others to establish and maintain enterprisewide cost controls.

Unsatisfactory

- Consistently fails to work within the established budget.
- Does not construct realistic and workable budgets.
- Does not demonstrate understanding of standard accounting principles.
- Does not keep within or below the allotted budget.
- Does not make good use of company resources.
- Does not use recognized principles of fiscal auditing.
- Fails to create realistic budget objectives.
- Fails to demonstrate ability to monitor cost accounting.
- Fails to demonstrate understanding of principles of cost accounting.
- Fails to develop reasonable budgets.
- Fails to control costs effectively.
- Fails to make the most of available funds and resources.
- Fails to monitor inventory levels to control costs.
- Fails to pay necessary attention to the bottom line.
- Fails to work with human resources to seek cost reductions through proper scheduling of work force.
- Has been unable to apply standard accounting principles to development and management of budgets.
- Has consistently gone beyond budgetary constraints.
- Has demonstrated an inability to effectively manage a budget.
- Has demonstrated an inability to establish realistic goals for the cost of manufacture.
- Has demonstrated an inability to establish realistic goals for the cost of services.
- Has demonstrated an inability to meet or stay below budgetary goals.

- Has failed to control and reduce travel and entertainment expenses adequately.
- Has failed to manage resources and staff adequately.
- Has failed to monitor travel and entertainment expenses in keeping with policy adequately.
- Has failed to manage variances from budget consistently.
- Has failed to consult with management about budget variances.
- Has failed to demonstrate close monitoring of variable costs.
- Has failed to demonstrate necessary financial expertise.
- Has failed to establish and maintain appropriate audit systems.
- Has failed to establish and maintain controls on expense accounts, including close monitoring of invoices and receipts.
- Has failed to identify new targets for cost reduction.
- Has failed to improve skills at developing realistic and efficient budgets.
- Has failed to seek ways to reduce costs without compromising quality.
- Has not demonstrated ability to make sound financial decisions.
- Has not demonstrated ability to properly analyze financial information.
- Has not demonstrated ability to provide management with accurate information on the cost of new procedures or policies.
- Has not shown ability to make appropriate operational decisions based on budgetary constraints.
- Has not sought new suppliers and contractors to reduce cost when appropriate.

- Has not sought to renegotiate contracts to reduce costs when appropriate.
- Has produced unacceptably inaccurate cost estimates.
- Is very uncomfortable in dealing with fiscal matters.
- Presents biased and unfair financial plans.
- Produces unrealistic and inefficient budgets.
- Unwilling to work with others to establish and maintain enterprisewide cost controls.

Knowledge of Job and Industry

Key Verbs

demonstrates
displays
shows
understands

Key Nouns

changes	history	requirements
enterprise	industry	responsibilities
expert	knowledge	scope

Meets or Exceeds

- Continuously seeks to learn of changes in the industry and enterprise and improve job performance.
- Demonstrates ability to anticipate changes in the industry.
- Demonstrates a firm grasp of the requirements of the job.
- Demonstrates an outstanding awareness of the complexities of the industry.

- Demonstrates strong understanding of basic management principles.
- Has a broad understanding of the needs of the job.
- Has an encyclopedic knowledge of the business and history of the industry.
- Keeps current on changing laws and regulations that affect the job.
- Keeps current on changing needs of the job and enterprise.
- Recognized in the enterprise as an expert.
- Recognized in the industry as an expert.
- Shares knowledge willingly and is considered the resident authority.
- Shows excellent knowledge of important departmental and enterprise guidelines and procedures
- Understands the scope of job responsibilities.

Needs Improvement

- Needs to become more familiar with all of the elements of the job description.
- Needs to demonstrate greater understanding of job responsibilities.
- Needs to improve knowledge of important departmental and enterprise guidelines and procedure.
- Needs to keep current on changing laws and regulations that affect the job.
- Needs to keep current on changing needs of the job and enterprise.
- Needs to work to keep current on changes in the industry and enterprise and improve job performance.
- Should become more familiar with specific job and industry.

- Should improve general understanding of the needs of the job.
- Should work to improve understanding of basic management principles.
- Thinking is too one-dimensional as it applies to the industry as a whole.

Unsatisfactory

- Does not demonstrate good understanding of job responsibilities.
- Does not have a grasp on the complexities of the job or the industry as a whole.
- Does not show understanding of basic management principles.
- Fails to keep current on changes in the industry and enterprise to improve job performance.
- Fails to keep current on changing laws and regulations that affect the job.
- Fails to keep current on changing needs of the job and enterprise.
- Fails to show general understanding of the needs of the job.
- Has demonstrated unwillingness to take steps necessary to understand requirements of the job.
- Has not shown knowledge of important departmental and enterprise guidelines and procedure.

Planning and Scheduling Skills

Key Verbs

accomplishes	demonstrates	plans
creates	makes	produces

Key Nouns

contingencies	preparation	responsibility
organization	relationships	strategy
plans		

Meets or Exceeds

- Ably brings together other departments and individuals in the development of strategic plans.
- Accomplishes assigned tasks within deadline.
- Accurately assesses needs in preparation for planning.
- Anticipates problems well.
- Brings innovation and fresh ideas to the planning process.
- Can quickly change direction when it is warranted.
- Creates workable plans for action.
- Cultivates relationships within the industry helpful to achieving goals.
- Demonstrates an ability to plan demand for resources and work force accurately.
- Demonstrates excellent ability to anticipate problems.
- Includes contingency plans for possible problems.
- Is not afraid of details.
- Is not intimidated by the complexity of a task.
- Makes carefully considered strategic plans.

- Produces effective plans that include contingency plans for unexpected problems.
- Produces plans quickly and efficiently.
- Produces plans that account for any contingency.
- Produces realistic and actionable strategic plans.
- Produces very effective strategic plans.
- Proposes realistic solutions to enterprise issues.
- Stays within allotted time for accomplishment of tasks.
- Uses superior organizational skills to the best advantage.
- Willingly accepts new responsibilities and assignments.
- Works closely with management to position the organization to take advantage of new opportunities.
- Works well with others in the development of strategic plans.
- Works well with others to merge needs and wants into effective and realistic plans.

Needs Improvement

- Needs to accomplish assigned tasks within deadline.
- Needs to become better organized.
- Needs to better demonstrate ability to plan demand for resources and work force accurately.
- Needs to handle the numerous details required of the job better.
- Needs to bring innovation and fresh ideas to the planning process.
- Needs to create workable plans for action.
- Needs to include contingency plans for possible problems.
- Needs to produce effective plans that include contingencies for unexpected problems.

- Needs to stay within allotted time for accomplishment of tasks.
- Needs to work better to bring together other departments and individuals in the development of strategic plans.
- Needs to work more closely with management to position the organization to take advantage of new opportunities.
- Should attempt to anticipate problems better.
- Should be more willing to accept new responsibilities and assignments.
- Should become more familiar with the differing needs of individual departments.
- Should cooperate with others to merge needs and wants into effective and realistic plans.
- Should consider strategic plans more carefully.
- Should work better with others in the development of strategic plans.
- Should work to better assess needs in preparation for planning.
- Should work to better demonstrate ability to anticipate problems.
- Should work to produce plans quickly and more efficiently.

Unsatisfactory

- Does not anticipate problems in drawing plans.
- Does not assess needs well in preparation for planning.
- Does not cooperate with others to merge needs and wants into effective and realistic plans.
- Does not succeed at bringing together other departments and individuals in the development of strategic plans.

- Fails to accomplish assigned tasks within deadline.
- Fails to anticipate problems.
- Fails to bring innovation and fresh ideas to the planning process.
- Fails to consider strategic plans carefully.
- Fails to include contingency plans for possible problems.
- Fails to produce effective plans that include contingency plans for unexpected problems.
- Fails to produce plans quickly and more efficiently.
- Fails to stay within allotted time for accomplishment of tasks.
- Fails to work closely with management to position the organization to take advantage of new opportunities.
- Has not demonstrated ability to plan demand for resources and work force accurately.
- Has not shown ability to work with others in the development of strategic plans.
- Has proved unable to focus on the details of critical assignments.
- Is overwhelmed and unorganized.
- Is unwilling to accept new responsibilities and assignments.
- Plans are not workable.

Setting Goals and Objectives

Key Verbs

    demonstrates
    establishes
    sets
    shows

Key Nouns and Adjectives

goals	objectives	realistic
objective measures	progress	targets

Meets or Exceeds

- Assists others in the setting of realistic goals for career advancement.
- Assists supervised staff in the setting of realistic personal goals for career advancement.
- Avoids setting unattainable goals.
- Communicates with supervisors and superiors about personal goals for career advancement.
- Demonstrates ability to evaluate progress toward goals.
- Establishes clearly defined goals allowing objective measurement of achievement.
- Establishes effective goals and objectives.
- Establishes effective goals and objectives for enterprise or department.
- Is very clear and focused when articulating objectives.
- Meets and exceeds personal goals and objectives.
- Meets with supervised staff to discuss and work to facilitate personal goals for career advancement.
- Sets and meets meaningful personal goals for career advancement.
- Sets practical and reasonable targets.
- Sets realistic and measurable goals for workgroups and departments.
- Sets realistic organizational and departmental goals.
- Sets realistic personal goals.

- Shows ability to visualize the finish line.
- Works to establish and fulfill short-term, mid-range, and long-term goals.
- Works to fulfill organizational goals as part of personal objectives.
- Works together with training staff to facilitate achievement of personal goals for supervised staff.

Needs Improvement

- Gives vague instructions and is not always clear when advising others of goals.
- Needs to set realistic personal goals.
- Needs to assist others in the setting of realistic goals for career advancement.
- Needs to better establish goals and objectives.
- Needs to establish and fulfill short-term, mid-range, and long-term goals.
- Needs to establish clearly defined goals allowing objective measurement of achievement.
- Needs to establish effective goals and objectives for enterprise or department.
- Needs to set realistic organizational and departmental goals.
- Needs to visualize the finish line.
- Should assist supervised staff in the setting of realistic personal goals for career advancement.
- Should communicate with supervisors and superiors about personal goals for career advancement.
- Should demonstrate ability to evaluate progress toward goals.

- Should include organizational goals as part of personal objectives.
- Should not set unattainable goals.
- Should regularly meet with supervised staff to discuss and work to facilitate goals for career advancement.
- Should set realistic and measurable goals for workgroups and departments.
- Should strive to meet and exceed personal goals and objectives.
- Should work to set and meet meaningful goals for career advancement.
- Should work together with training staff to facilitate achievement of personal goals for supervised staff.
- Tends to overreach and set unattainable targets.

Unsatisfactory

- Does not establish and fulfill short-term, mid-range, and long-term goals.
- Does not regularly meet with supervised staff to discuss and work to facilitate goals for career advancement.
- Does not seem capable of fully understanding goals.
- Fails to assist others in the setting of realistic goals for career advancement.
- Fails to assist supervised staff in the setting of realistic personal goals for career advancement.
- Fails to include organizational goals as part of personal objectives.
- Fails to set and meet meaningful goals for career advancement.
- Fails to set realistic organizational and departmental goals.

- Fails to set realistic personal goals.
- Has been unable to meet personal goals and objectives.
- Has failed to communicate with supervisors and superiors about personal goals for career advancement.
- Has failed to set realistic and measurable goals for work-groups and departments.
- Has not cooperated with training staff to facilitate achievement of personal goals for supervised staff.
- Has not demonstrated ability to evaluate progress toward goals.
- Has not established clearly defined goals allowing objective measurement of achievement.
- Sets unlikely and out-of-reach targets.
- Unable to establish effective goals and objectives.
- Unable to establish effective goals and objectives for enterprise or department.

Technical Competence

Key Verbs

demonstrates
develops
produces
understands

Key Nouns

competence	task forces	technologies
documentation	teams	training

Meets or Exceeds

- Continuously seeks advanced training on job-related technical skills.
- Demonstrates strong understanding of technical requirements of the job.
- Demonstrates thorough understanding of computer technology and applies them to job tasks.
- Develops and maintains effective technical teams.
- Is a proven and effective manager of technical teams and task forces.
- Is meticulous in preparation and highly accurate.
- Keeps current on changing technologies and trends.
- Produces clear and direct technical documentation.
- Takes advantage of available training and tools to maintain and enhance technical skills.
- Understands the mechanics of an operation.
- Works closely with other departments to promote introduction of new technologies to improve productivity, boost quality, and reduce costs.
- Works closely with other departments to raise awareness of technical issues.
- Works closely with quality control to coordinate technical efforts with organizational goals.
- Works well with individuals and teams to further technical goals.

Needs Improvement

- Is sometimes overwhelmed by the mechanics of an operation.
- Must develop and maintain effective technical teams.

- Must improve skills to be an effective manager of technical teams and task forces.
- Must keep current on changing technologies and trends.
- Must work more closely with quality control to coordinate technical efforts with organizational goals.
- Needs to better demonstrate strong understanding of technical requirements of the job.
- Needs to improve ability to work well with individuals and teams to further technical goals.
- Needs to improve skills to produce clear and direct technical documentation.
- Needs to work closely with other departments to raise awareness of technical issues.
- Needs to work more closely with other departments to promote introduction of new technologies to improve productivity, boost quality, and reduce costs.
- Should strive to demonstrate thorough understanding of computer technology and apply it to job tasks.
- Should seek advanced training on job-related technical skills.
- Should take advantage of available training and tools to maintain and enhance technical skills.
- Tends to be careless and inaccurate.

Unsatisfactory

- Does not demonstrate strong understanding of technical requirements of the job.
- Fails to demonstrate thorough understanding of computer technology and apply it to job tasks.
- Fails to keep current on changing technologies and trends.

- Fails to seek advanced training on job-related technical skills.
- Fails to work closely with other departments to promote introduction of new technologies to improve productivity, boost quality, and reduce costs.
- Fails to work closely with other departments to raise awareness of technical issues.
- Has failed to develop and maintain effective technical teams.
- Has failed to work well with individuals and teams to further technical goals.
- Has not demonstrated capabilities as a proven and effective manager of technical teams and task forces.
- Has not shown ability to produce clear and direct technical documentation.
- Has not shown ability to work closely with quality control to coordinate technical efforts with organizational goals.
- Has turned down opportunities to take advantage of available training and tools to maintain and enhance technical skills.
- Work is filled with errors.

Time Management and Prioritization

Key Verbs

demonstrates	handles	meets
displays	manages	prioritizes

Key Nouns

assignments	projects	strategies
deadlines	resources	tasks
priorities		

Meets or Exceeds

- Able to manage multiple assignments.
- Can accurately access the time required for a particular task.
- Capably handles competitive priorities.
- Consistently meets or beats deadlines.
- Demonstrates ability to identify projects and strategies that waste time and resources.
- Demonstrates ability to manage use of resources and staff to accomplish prioritized tasks.
- Demonstrates ability to prioritize assignments.
- Demonstrates excellent time-management skills.
- Displays strong skills at delegation of tasks to maximize productivity.
- Effectively manages resources and staff as part of time-management and prioritization strategy.
- Effectively prioritizes tasks to meet organizational goals.
- Focuses on highest priority tasks while maintaining progress on other assignments.
- Is able to manage multiple priorities with differing demands on resources and staff effectively.
- Is able to multitask successfully.
- Keeps supervisors informed of progress toward completion of multiple tasks.

- Makes the best use of available time and resources.
- Manages multiple assignments well.
- Prioritizes tasks well.
- Sets realistic and efficient deadlines and goals.
- Understands the varying priority of different tasks.
- Works well with multiple supervisors.
- Works well with other individuals and departments to make the most of available time and resources to accomplish goals.
- Works well with supervised staff to prioritize tasks.
- Works with managers to eliminate non-essential tasks.

Needs Improvement

- Has difficulty handling more than one task at a time.
- Must improve ability to prioritize assignments.
- Must strive to better manage multiple assignments.
- Needs to be more realistic and efficient in setting deadlines and goals.
- Needs to become more skilled at prioritizing tasks to meet organizational goals.
- Needs to better identify projects and strategies that waste time and resources.
- Needs to demonstrate ability to manage multiple assignments.
- Needs to improve ability to manage use of resources and staff to accomplish prioritized tasks.
- Needs to improve ability to prioritize tasks.
- Needs to improve ability to work with managers to eliminate non-essential tasks.
- Needs to improve ability to work with supervised staff to prioritize tasks.

- Needs to improve skills at delegation of tasks to maximize productivity.
- Needs to improve skills at time management.
- Needs to improve the use of available time and resources.
- Needs to keep supervisors informed of progress toward completion of multiple tasks.
- Needs to learn to focus on highest priority tasks while maintaining progress on other assignments.
- Needs to learn to put multiple tasks in order of priority.
- Needs to learn to work well with multiple supervisors.
- Needs to meet deadlines more consistently.
- Needs to manage resources and staff more effectively as part of time management and prioritization strategy.
- Should improve ability to manage multiple priorities with differing demands on resources and staff effectively.
- Should improve ability to work well with other individuals and departments to make the most of available time and resources to accomplish goals.
- Should strive to better handle competitive priorities.
- Should work on skills to determine the length of time required to complete different tasks.

Unsatisfactory

- Consistently fails to meet deadlines.
- Does not effectively manage resources and staff as part of time management and prioritization strategy.
- Does not handle competitive priorities well.
- Does not demonstrate understanding of how to put tasks in order of priority.

- Does not work well with other individuals and departments to make the most of available time and resources to accomplish goals.
- Does not work with managers to eliminate non-essential tasks.
- Fails to delegate tasks effectively to maximize productivity.
- Fails to prioritize tasks effectively to meet organizational goals.
- Fails to keep supervisors informed of progress toward completion of multiple tasks.
- Fails to make good use of available time and resources.
- Fails to manage multiple assignments well.
- Fails to prioritize tasks properly.
- Fails to work well with multiple supervisors.
- Fails to work with supervised staff to prioritize tasks.
- Has failed to demonstrate ability to identify projects and strategies that waste time and resources.
- Has failed to demonstrate ability to manage multiple assignments.
- Has failed to focus on highest priority tasks while maintaining progress on other assignments.
- Has failed to demonstrate ability to prioritize assignments.
- Has not demonstrated ability to manage multiple priorities with differing demands on resources and staff effectively.
- Has not demonstrated effective skills in time management.
- Has not demonstrated the ability to multitask.
- Has not shown ability to manage use of resources and staff to accomplish prioritized tasks.
- Has proved unable to determine required time to complete tasks.
- Is unrealistic and inefficient in setting deadlines and goals.

Work Habits, Punctuality, and Attendance

Key Verbs

follows
displays
meets

Key Nouns

deadlines	professionalism	role model
organization	records	tasks

Meets or Exceeds

- Completes tasks in a timely manner.
- Consistently exceeds goals.
- Follows scheduled arrival and departure time.
- Has an excellent attendance record.
- Is highly organized at work.
- Meets or exceeds deadlines.

Needs Improvement

- Asks for too many extensions in completing tasks.
- Consistently falls short of goals.
- Is not dependable.
- Is not timely in meeting goals.
- Must make arrangements to permit meeting scheduled arrival and departure time.
- Needs to become more organized at work.
- Needs to regularly meet or exceed deadlines.
- Should work on improving attendance record.

Unsatisfactory

- Consistently falls short of goals.
- Does not have a good attendance record.
- Does not regularly follow scheduled arrival and departure time.
- Does not regularly meet or exceed deadlines.
- Fails to demonstrate skills in organizing work.
- Has failed to demonstrate ability to follow the rules.
- Has missed work for unexcused reasons (X) times.
- Has proved unable to meet goals.

Chapter 7

MANAGEMENT SKILLS

EVALUATING A MANAGER can seem a bit like nailing Jell-O to the wall. Does a supervisor deserve the blame for the failure of someone on the staff? Can the same supervisor claim the credit for another's success? The answer is yes to both questions—but the manager must be held to criteria that are clearly laid out in a job description and consistently applied to everyone with the same duties and responsibilities.

- Administrative skills
- Delegating tasks
- Employee evaluation and performance appraisal skills
- Environmental management
- Job safety and security management
- Leadership skills
- Management skills
- Organizational skills
- Productivity
- Sales management
- Supervisory skills
- Training and employee development skills

Administrative Skills

Key Verbs

administers	establishes	oversees
demonstrates	manages	

Key Nouns

administrative support	professional responsibilities
efficiency	record retention
management of records	records
organizational skills	statistical analysis
personnel records	technology
procedures	time management

Meets or Exceeds

- Able to separate personal issues from professional responsibilities effectively.
- Administers department with exceptional skill.
- Contributes to improvement in administrative procedures companywide.
- Demonstrated ability to handle increased load of information and records.
- Demonstrates an excellent understanding of current administrative methods.
- Demonstrates excellent organizational skills.
- Demonstrates leadership capacity.
- Demonstrates understanding of statistical analysis tools.
- Efficiently oversees collection and management of records.
- Establishes clear and understandable administrative rules.

- Establishes plans to reduce paperwork and improve access to information.
- Establishes valuable administrative support systems to improve productivity.
- Is highly competent in administrative tasks.
- Is highly productive.
- Is an excellent mediator, capable of resolving conflicts before they escalate.
- Keeps management informed of administrative accomplishments and goals.
- Maintains the confidentiality of personnel records with great skill.
- Makes excellent use of forms to improve efficiency and reduce paperwork.
- Makes good use of office technology in the performance of administrative duties.
- Manages department filing with skill.
- Manages electronic records with great skill.
- Manages proprietary information properly.
- Manages record retention properly, meeting legal, tax, and corporate needs.
- Manages the flow of paperwork very well.
- Oversees a continuing improvement in information retrieval processes.
- Oversees administrative tasks with minimal demands on management.
- Oversees an efficient and up-to-date filing system.
- Seeks improved administrative procedures and goals.
- Seeks improved efficiency in administrative procedures.
- Seeks out new policies and procedures for department.

- Studies and implements new technologies to improve administrative functions.
- Well organized and uses time efficiently.

Needs Improvement

- Must improve management of the confidentiality of personnel records.
- Needs to address ways to deal with the increasing load of information and records.
- Needs to be more proactive in anticipating conflicts before they escalate.
- Needs to better maintain balance of personal obligations and professional demands.
- Needs to consider increased use of forms to improve efficiency and reduce paperwork.
- Needs to consider new policies and procedures where appropriate.
- Needs to consider ways to improve efficiency in administrative procedures.
- Needs to develop clearer and more understandable administrative rules.
- Needs to develop improved administrative support systems for better productivity.
- Needs to find ways to deal with the increasing flow of paperwork.
- Needs to find ways to improve efficiency in collecting and managing records.
- Needs to improve administrative skills.
- Needs to improve departmental filing.
- Needs to improve organizational skills.

- Needs to improve productivity rate.
- Needs to improve record retention procedures to meet legal, tax, and corporate needs.
- Needs to improve skills with statistical analysis tools.
- Needs to improve the filing system to make it more efficient and up-to-date.
- Needs to improve the use of office technology in the performance of administrative duties.
- Needs to improve understanding of current administrative methods.
- Needs to improve management of proprietary information.
- Needs to seek new administrative procedures and goals where appropriate.
- Needs to study new technologies for use in administrative functions.
- Should be less demanding of management in overseeing administrative tasks.
- Should consider contributing to improvements in administrative procedures companywide.
- Should consider means to reduce paperwork and improve access to information.
- Should devote more effort to effective management of electronic records.
- Should keep management better informed of administrative accomplishments and goals.
- Should make better use of time.
- Should work to improve information retrieval processes.

Unsatisfactory

- Delivers below-average productivity.
- Delivers weak administrative skills.
- Demonstrates failure to handle duties as defined in job description.
- Demonstrates unacceptable administrative skills.
- Demonstrates unacceptable organizational skills.
- Fails to address the increasing load of information and records.
- Fails to keep the filing system up-to-date.
- Fails to seek training on current administrative methods.
- Fails to address information retrieval problems.
- Fails to inform management adequately of administrative accomplishments and goals.
- Fails to manage departmental filing needs adequately.
- Fails to manage record retention of important legal, tax, and corporate information adequately.
- Fails to be proactive in anticipating disputes in order to avoid interdepartmental turmoil.
- Fails to consider new policies and procedures where appropriate.
- Fails to contribute new administrative procedures and goals where appropriate.
- Fails to contribute to paperwork reduction and improved access to information.
- Fails to develop clear and understandable administrative rules.
- Fails to develop improved administrative support systems for better productivity.
- Fails to keep current with new technologies that could improve administrative functions.

- Fails to make adequate use of office technology in the performance of administrative duties.
- Fails to oversee management of proprietary information properly.
- Fails to seek ways to improve efficiency in administrative procedures.
- Has demonstrated inability to separate personal and professional obligations.
- Has failed to effectively manage electronic records.
- Has not dealt with the increasing flow of paperwork.
- Has not made use of forms to improve efficiency and reduce paperwork.
- Unable to deal with increasing load of information and records.
- Unable to improve efficiency in collecting and managing records.
- Unable to make good use of statistical analysis tools.
- Unable to safeguard the confidentiality of personnel records.
- Unnecessarily involves management in oversight of administrative tasks.
- Unwilling to contribute to companywide administrative improvements.

Delegating Tasks

Key Verbs

| allows | demonstrates | maintains |
| delegates | judges | |

Key Nouns and Adjectives

allocation
authority
capabilities
delegated tasks

delegation
effective
follow-up
insight

instructions
judges
responsibility

Meets or Exceeds

- Is a good judge of others' capabilities.
- Allows supervised staff the authority to fulfill delegated tasks.
- Carefully follows up after allocation of tasks.
- Carefully matches delegated tasks to appropriate supervised staff.
- Delegates effectively.
- Demonstrates proper judgment in selecting tasks for delegation.
- Effectively uses delegation as means to expand employee capabilities and enhance productivity.
- Encourages coworkers to delegate tasks where appropriate.
- Encourages supervised staff to seek more responsibility.
- Gives supervised staff clear instructions and authority to accomplish delegated tasks.
- Has a demeanor that encourages personal responsibility by staffers.
- Maintains appropriate oversight of delegated tasks.
- Shows a great deal of insight in fitting individuals to tasks.
- Is well respected by supervised staff.
- Is worthy of being delegated for more demanding and responsible assignments.

Needs Improvement

- Demeanor does not encourage personal responsibility in staffers.
- Needs to allow supervised staff the authority to fulfill delegated tasks.
- Needs to be more informed about complexities of task before attempting to delegate.
- Needs to encourage supervised staff to seek more responsibility.
- Needs to follow up with appropriate staff after delegation of tasks.
- Needs to give supervised staff clear instructions and authority to accomplish delegated tasks.
- Needs to improve ability to delegate tasks.
- Needs to improve ability to judge capabilities of others.
- Needs to improve judgment in selecting tasks for delegation.
- Needs to maintain appropriate oversight of delegated tasks.
- Needs to more carefully match delegated tasks to appropriate supervised staff.
- Should encourage coworkers to delegate tasks where appropriate.
- Should learn to use delegation as means to expand employee capabilities and enhance productivity.

Unsatisfactory

- By personal example, does not encourage personal responsibility in staff.
- Demonstrates poor judgment in assignment of delegated tasks.

- Does not match delegated tasks to appropriate supervised staff.
- Fails to delegate tasks appropriately.
- Fails to give supervised staff clear instructions and authority to accomplish delegated tasks.
- Fails to maintain appropriate oversight of delegated tasks.
- Gives unclear messages to subordinates about expected outcome.
- Has not allowed supervised staff the authority to fulfill delegated tasks.
- Has not encouraged coworkers to delegate tasks where appropriate.
- Is not timely enough in delegating responsibilities, reducing time for completion of assignments and quality of output.
- Is too hasty in delegating responsibilities, resulting in inappropriate choices.
- Once a task is delegated, does not monitor progress.
- Once a task is delegated, refuses to surrender responsibility to staff.
- Uses poor judgment in selecting tasks for delegation.

Employee Evaluation and Performance Appraisal Skills

Key Verbs

demonstrates	establishes	oversees
develops	maintains	

Key Nouns

advancement	fairness	potential
appraisals	guidelines	promotion
assessments	measurements	reaction
capabilities	motivation	requirements
criteria	objectives	training
evaluations	performance	

Meets or Exceeds

- Anticipates employee reactions to performance appraisals.
- Carefully plans for performance appraisals.
- Clearly demonstrates unbiased, objective criteria for performance appraisals.
- Clearly links salary increases to objective employee appraisals.
- Continuously updates and modifies criteria and objectives for performance appraisals and evaluations.
- Demonstrates ability to produce effective and true assessments.
- Demonstrates ability to recognize employees with untapped potential.
- Demonstrates ability to uncover unrecognized potential and capabilities in employees.
- Demonstrates fairness in criteria for performance appraisals.
- Demonstrates fairness in gauging performance against objective criteria.
- Demonstrates understanding of legal requirements and enterprise guidelines for performance appraisals.

- Demonstrates willingness to properly note responses from employees undergoing performance appraisal.
- Develops clear criteria and objectives for performance appraisals and evaluations.
- Develops objective measurements for job performance.
- Does not have a personal agenda.
- Encourages employees to use performance appraisal for career advancement.
- Has a proven record of recognizing exceptional performance.
- Has demonstrated over time that performance appraisals accurately track the capabilities and potential of employees.
- Is able to anticipate a potential problem before it gets out of hand.
- Is able to maintain a professional relationship with employees while remaining approachable.
- Is known as a fair evaluator.
- Makes effective use of performance appraisals and evaluations to motivate employees.
- Oversees conduct of unbiased, objective performance appraisals.
- Provides appropriate documentation for observations in performance appraisals.
- Works closely with human resources department to develop and maintain appropriate performance appraisal criteria.
- Works closely with trainers to identify employees in need of job training and career advancement.

Needs Improvement

- Is perceived as allowing personal preferences to affect evaluations.
- Needs to be more approachable and informed about potential personnel situations.
- Needs to demonstrate fairness in criteria for performance appraisals clearly.
- Needs to link salary increases to objective employee appraisals clearly.
- Needs to produce unbiased, objective performance appraisals consistently.
- Needs to demonstrate ability to produce effective and true assessments.
- Needs to demonstrate fairness in gauging performance against objective criteria.
- Needs to demonstrate over time that performance appraisals accurately track capabilities and potential of employees.
- Needs to demonstrate understanding of legal requirements and enterprise guidelines for performance appraisals.
- Needs to develop clear criteria and objectives for performance appraisals and evaluations.
- Needs to provide appropriate documentation for observations in performance appraisals.
- Needs to update and modify criteria and objectives for performance appraisals and evaluations regularly.
- On occasion, a personal agenda seems evident.
- Should better anticipate employee reactions to performance appraisals.
- Should carefully plan for performance appraisals.

- Should demonstrate willingness to properly note responses from employees undergoing performance appraisal.
- Should develop objective measurements for job performance.
- Should encourage employees to use performance appraisal for career advancement.
- Should strive to avoid the appearance of favoritism in issuing appraisal evaluations.
- Should strive to demonstrate ability to uncover unrecognized potential and capabilities in employees.
- Should strive to demonstrate unbiased, objective criteria for performance appraisals.
- Should strive to make effective use of performance appraisals and evaluations to motivate employees.
- Should strive to recognize employees with untapped potential.
- Should strive to recognize exceptional performance.
- Should work closely with trainers to identify employees in need of job training and career advancement.
- Should work more closely with human resources department to develop and maintain appropriate performance appraisal criteria.

Unsatisfactory

- Coworkers do not have faith they will receive an unbiased appraisal.
- Does not carefully plan for performance appraisals.
- Does not make effective use of performance appraisals and evaluations to motivate employees.
- Does not recognize the need for confidentiality in issuing performance evaluations.

- Fails to anticipate employee reactions to performance appraisals.
- Fails to avoid the appearance of favoritism in issuing performance appraisals.
- Fails to link salary increases to objective employee appraisals clearly.
- Fails to demonstrate fairness in criteria for performance appraisals.
- Fails to demonstrate fairness in gauging performance against objective criteria.
- Fails to demonstrate unbiased, objective criteria for performance appraisals.
- Fails to demonstrate understanding of legal requirements and enterprise guidelines for performance appraisals.
- Fails to develop clear criteria and objectives for performance appraisals and evaluations.
- Fails to develop objective measurements for job performance.
- Fails to encourage employees to use performance appraisal for career advancement.
- Fails to note responses from employees undergoing performance appraisal properly.
- Fails to provide appropriate documentation for observations in performance appraisals.
- Fails to update and modify criteria and objectives for performance appraisals and evaluations regularly.
- Fails to work closely with human resources department to develop and maintain appropriate performance appraisal criteria.
- Has failed to demonstrate ability to produce effective and true assessments.

- Has failed to demonstrate ability to uncover unrecognized potential and capabilities in employees.
- Has failed to demonstrate over time that performance appraisals accurately track capabilities and potential of employees.
- Has failed to work closely with trainers to identify employees in need of job training and career advancement.
- Has maintained an unapproachable and remote attitude with employees.
- Has not consistently produced unbiased, objective performance appraisals.
- Is perceived as having a personal stake in outcome of evaluations.
- Violates legal requirements and enterprise guidelines for performance appraisals.

Environmental Management

Key Verbs

conveys
devotes
works

Key Nouns

agencies	guidelines	regulations
education	insurance carriers	training

Meets or Exceeds

- Is able to convey to coworkers the importance of environmental issues in their professional and personal lives.
- Devotes appropriate time to education and training on environmental issues.
- Is able to deliver a message that is perceived as sincere.
- Is able to convey the importance of an issue by example.
- Keeps current on environmental regulations and guidelines.
- Works closely with governmental agencies and insurance carriers to enforce environmental regulations and guidelines.

Needs Improvement

- Does not convey to coworkers the importance of environmental issues outside the workplace.
- Needs to keep current on environmental regulations and guidelines.
- Needs to set a more positive example regarding the importance of an issue.
- Presents an image that is in contrast to professional status.
- Should devote appropriate time to education and training on environmental issues.
- Should work more closely with governmental agencies and insurance carriers to enforce environmental regulations and guidelines.

Unsatisfactory

- Conveys the attitude that matters relating to the environment are unnecessary intrusions.
- Does not convey by example the importance of an issue.

- Fails to devote appropriate time to education and training on environmental issues.
- Fails to keep current on environmental regulations and guidelines.
- Has failed to work closely with governmental agencies and insurance carriers to enforce environmental regulations and guidelines.

Job Safety and Security Management

Key Verbs

devotes	follows	meets
exceeds	maintains	

Key Nouns

attitude	education	security
concerns	prevention	training
coordination	safety	

Meets or Exceeds

- Consistently follows safety and security recommendations.
- Conveys an attitude to coworkers that is reassuring and supportive.
- Coordinates enterprise security with local homeland defense agencies.
- Devotes appropriate time to education and training on safety and security issues.
- Devotes full effort to monitoring new safety concerns and programs.

- Diligently follows safety guidelines and regulations.
- Effectively coordinates enterprise safety and security programs with local authorities.
- Effectively works with insurance carrier and state agencies to manage occupational safety programs.
- Encourages enterprisewide campaign to uncover safety concerns.
- Has developed and maintained effective emergency evacuation plans in cooperation with area authorities.
- Is consistently up-to-date on changes in regulations and laws.
- Is open and willing to hear concerns and ideas of coworkers.
- Keeps abreast of new security measures and devices.
- Maintains an effective accident prevention program.
- Works closely with security officials to monitor visitors and suppliers.

Needs Improvement

- Does not adequately communicate to employees a sense of workplace safety.
- Does not reach out to coworkers for suggestions and concerns.
- Fails to keep abreast of new security measures and devices.
- Fails to keep current with new laws and regulations.
- Needs to be more consistent in following safety and security recommendations.
- Needs to better coordinate efforts with insurance carrier and state agencies to manage occupational safety programs.

- Needs to coordinate enterprise security with local homeland defense agencies.
- Needs to develop and maintain effective emergency evacuation plans in cooperation with area authorities.
- Needs to devote appropriate time to education and training on safety and security issues.
- Needs to devote more effort to monitoring new safety concerns and programs.
- Needs to improve compliance with safety guidelines and regulations.
- Should establish and maintain an effective accident prevention program.
- Should establish enterprisewide campaign to uncover safety concerns.
- Should work more closely with security officials to monitor visitors and suppliers.
- Should work to better coordinate enterprise safety and security programs with local authorities.

Unsatisfactory

- Does not instill in employees confidence that workplace is safe and secure.
- Fails to comply with safety guidelines and regulations.
- Fails to coordinate enterprise safety and security programs with local authorities.
- Fails to coordinate with security officials to monitor visitors and suppliers.
- Fails to follow safety and security recommendations.
- Fails to monitor new safety concerns and programs.
- Has failed to coordinate enterprise security with local

homcland defense agencies.
- Has failed to develop and maintain effective emergency evacuation plans in cooperation with area authorities.
- Has failed to establish an effective accident prevention program.
- Has not coordinated with insurance carrier and state agencies to manage occupational safety programs.
- Has not devoted appropriate time to education and training on safety and security issues.
- Is not approachable for suggestions and concerns from coworkers.
- Is not capable of keeping up-to-date on new laws and regulations.
- Is not capable of keeping abreast of new security measures and devices.

Leadership Skills

Key Verbs

demonstrates
displays
inspires
shows

Key Nouns

common goals	example	role model
confidence	goals	self-assurance
creativity	recognition	vision
enthusiasm	respect	

Meets or Exceeds

- Brings individuals and groups together to accomplish common goals.
- Builds high morale and spirit among staff.
- Communicates self-assurance and encourages confidence in employees.
- Demonstrates appropriate leadership styles in varying circumstances.
- Demonstrates willingness to lead.
- Displays appropriate self-confidence and enthusiasm.
- Displays decisive and firm leadership when appropriate.
- Displays great vision and creativity as a leader.
- Effectively deals with disputes among staff.
- Inspires others by the quality of leadership shown.
- Is a natural leader, respected by supervised staff.
- Is a strong and visionary leader.
- Is not afraid of taking on the task of acting as a role model.
- Is recognized by others as a worthy leader.
- Is respected as a leader.
- Is respected by supervised staff.
- Knows the territory.
- Leads by example.
- Shows leadership by example.
- Shows natural leadership qualities.

Needs Improvement

- Must learn the complexities of the job before attempting to supervise others.
- Needs to adapt leadership style to varying circumstances.
- Needs to improve leadership skills.

- Needs to deal more effectively with disputes among staff.
- Needs to work to bring together individuals and groups to accomplish common goals.
- Should be more decisive and firm as a leader when appropriate.
- Should demonstrate willingness to lead.
- Should display more self-confidence and enthusiasm.
- Should show leadership by example.
- Should work to build high morale and spirit among staff.
- Should work to garner the respect of supervised staff.

Unsatisfactory

- Does not address issues of low morale among staff.
- Does not demonstrate willingness to lead.
- Does not display self-confidence or enthusiasm in performance of job duties.
- Does not effectively deal with disputes.
- Does not inspire self-assurance and confidence among coworkers.
- Does not show leadership skills.
- Fails to adapt leadership style to varying circumstances.
- Fails to bring individuals and groups together to accomplish common goals.
- Fails to build high morale and spirit among staff.
- Fails to show leadership by example.
- Fails to show vision and creativity as a leader.
- Has demonstrated an inability to communicate the needs of the job because of a lack of understanding of its complexities.
- Is an uncomfortable and ineffective leader.

- Is not respected as a leader.
- Needs to garner the respect of supervised staff.

Management Skills

Key Verbs

demonstrates
displays
manages
shows

Key Nouns

accountability	instructions	reports
assignments	issues	respect
budget	principles	salary
change	procedures	status
compassion	process	superiors
consultants	productivity	supervised staff
effectiveness	programs	supervisors
guidance	promotion	tracking

Meets or Exceeds

- Appropriately keeps supervisors informed on status of management issues.
- Appropriately seeks assistance from consultants and supervisors.
- Appropriately ties promotion and salary increases to job performance.
- Assists supervised staff in adjusting to change.

- Closely follows guidelines and regulations for employee supervision.
- Delivers accurate and valuable information to human resources department.
- Delivers clear and concise instructions to supervised staff.
- Delivers clear and effective reports to supervisors.
- Demonstrates ability to adapt to changing situations.
- Demonstrates ability to develop management programs to deal with problems.
- Demonstrates ability to implement changes without disruption.
- Demonstrates excellent budgeting skills.
- Demonstrates excellent human resources management skills.
- Demonstrates productive use of management principles and procedures.
- Demonstrates respect for employees.
- Demonstrates strong ability to stay within departmental or enterprise budget.
- Demonstrates strong understanding of management principles.
- Develops and oversees effective management programs.
- Displays excellent ability to identify management needs.
- Effectively applies principles of management to job assignment.
- Effectively brings together various departments for common effort.
- Effectively follows policies and guidelines.
- Encourages productive change to procedures.
- Encourages supervised staff to contribute to management process.

- Gains a high degree of productivity from staff.
- Handles crises well.
- Handles employee performance appraisals with great skill.
- Is a valuable management asset of the organization.
- Is able to maintain control in a crisis.
- Is able to maintain control over all aspects of an operation.
- Is an effective supervisor.
- Is capable of keeping track of a task from inception to completion.
- Is well respected as a manager.
- Keeps supervisors advised of obstacles to expected performance.
- Maintains appropriate documentation of managerial actions in keeping with policies.
- Makes excellent use of available resources and facilities.
- Manages ongoing programs effectively and efficiently.
- Manages staff effectively and compassionately.
- Manages well in a crisis.
- Motivates employees through effective performance appraisals.
- Oversees operational changes well.
- Provides supervised staff with the necessary authority and resources to accomplish assignments.
- Requires appropriate accountability from supervised staff.
- Seeks and receives management support for programs where appropriate.
- Seeks guidance from supervisors when appropriate.
- Works well in joint efforts with other departments.
- Works well with employees working in remote locations.
- Works well with other departments to resolve conflicts.

Needs Improvement

- Does not follow up with appropriate staffers on status of an assignment.
- Must work to enhance understanding and maintain control over all parts of an operation.
- Needs to tie promotion and salary increases appropriately to job performance.
- Needs to become a more effective supervisor.
- Needs to better manage ongoing programs.
- Needs to better provide staff with the necessary authority and resources to accomplish assignments.
- Needs to demonstrate a strong understanding of management principles.
- Needs to demonstrate ability to better handle crises.
- Needs to demonstrate ability to stay within departmental or enterprise budget.
- Needs to demonstrate better ability to follow policies and guidelines.
- Needs to improve ability to make operational changes.
- Needs to improve ability to manage staff effectively and compassionately.
- Needs to improve ability to work together in joint efforts with other departments.
- Needs to improve budgeting skills.
- Needs to improve skills for employee performance appraisals.
- Needs to improve supervision of employees working in remote locations.
- Needs to improve the quality of information and feedback provided to human resources department.

- Needs to keep better track of delegated work.
- Needs to keep supervisors better informed on status of management issues.
- Needs to make better use of available resources and facilities.
- Needs to more closely follow guidelines and regulations for employee supervision.
- Needs to require appropriate accountability of supervised staff.
- Should better demonstrate ability to adapt to changing situations.
- Should encourage productive changes to procedures.
- Should encourage supervised staff to contribute to management process.
- Should improve ability to deliver clear and effective reports to supervisors.
- Should keep supervisors advised of obstacles to expected performance.
- Should provide better documentation of managerial actions in keeping with policies.
- Should seek and receive management support for programs where appropriate.
- Should seek assistance from consultants and supervisors when appropriate.
- Should seek guidance from supervisors when appropriate.
- Should show more respect for employees.
- Should strive to develop and oversee effective management programs.
- Should strive to develop management programs to deal with problems.

- Should strive to use performance appraisals to motivate employees.
- Should strive to work better with other departments to resolve conflicts.
- Should work to assist supervised staff in adjusting to change.
- Should work to bring together various departments for common effort.
- Should work to identify management needs.
- Should work to improve ability to deliver clear and concise instructions to supervised staff.
- Should work to improve human resources management skills.
- Should work to improve productivity by supervised staff.
- Should work to more effectively apply principles of management to job assignments.

Unsatisfactory

- Displays inadequate human resources management skills.
- Does not deliver clear and effective reports to supervisors.
- Does not demonstrate acceptable budgeting skills.
- Does not effectively use performance appraisals to motivate employees.
- Does not encourage supervised staff to contribute to management process.
- Does not handle implementation of operational changes well.
- Does not require appropriate accountability of supervised staff.
- Does not successfully bring together various departments for common effort.
- Fails to deliver clear and concise instructions to supervised staff.

- Fails to demonstrate a strong understanding of management principles.
- Fails to keep supervisors adequately informed on status of management issues.
- Fails to keep supervisors advised of obstacles to expected performance.
- Fails to maintain control and authority over all parts of an operation.
- Fails to maintain proper documentation of managerial actions, in violation of policies.
- Fails to make full use of available resources and facilities in performance of job responsibilities.
- Fails to manage well in a crisis.
- Fails to seek assistance from consultants and supervisors when appropriate.
- Fails to seek guidance from supervisors when appropriate.
- Has been unable to adequately supervise employees working in remote locations.
- Has demonstrated an inability to provide staff with the necessary authority and resources to accomplish assignments.
- Has demonstrated an inability to stay within departmental or enterprise budget.
- Has demonstrated inability to closely follow guidelines and regulations for employee supervision.
- Has demonstrated inability to follow policies and guidelines.
- Has demonstrated inability to maintain control in a crisis.
- Has demonstrated inadequate skills for employee performance appraisals.
- Has demonstrated inappropriate or inadequate handling of employee performance appraisals.

- Has failed to demonstrate ability to adapt to changing situations.
- Has failed to provide accurate and effective information to human resources department.
- Has not appropriately tied promotion and salary increases to job performance.
- Has not demonstrated ability to be an effective supervisor.
- Has not demonstrated ability to improve productivity of supervised staff.
- Has not shown ability to work together in joint efforts with other departments.
- Has not worked well with other departments to resolve conflicts.
- Has shown no ability to follow up with staffers on status of an assignment.
- Is not well respected as a manager by supervised staff.
- Loses track of tasks once they are delegated.

Organizational Skills

Key Verbs

assists	leads	shows
demonstrates	manages	

Key Nouns

maximization	preparation	staffing levels
methodology	priorities	workload
planning	reorganization	

Meets or Exceeds

- Assists the organization in determining proper staffing levels.
- Is consistently well organized and prepared for any eventuality.
- Deals well with reorganization programs.
- Demonstrates excellent organizational skills.
- Demonstrates excellent skills in organizing projects and workload.
- Has demonstrated great accuracy in determining staffing needs.
- Helps the enterprise improve productivity through improved organization.
- Is a methodical planner and organizer.
- Is able to control a situation effectively because of sharp organizational abilities.
- Is able to put priorities in perspective when emergencies arise.
- Is an extremely well organized worker.
- Is consistently up-to-date on changes in staffing needs.
- Leads effective departmental reorganization efforts.
- Manages departmental reorganization efforts well.
- Shows ability to help maximize the use of staff.

Needs Improvement

- Does not impress others in dealings because of apparent confusion about task.
- Does not keep current with staffing needs and changes.
- Needs to be prepared for emergencies and the resulting changes.
- Needs to manage the organizing of projects and workload better.

- Needs to improve accuracy in determining staffing needs.
- Needs to improve organizational skills.
- Needs to improve skills to deal with reorganization programs.
- Should work to assist in determining proper staffing levels.
- Should work to help maximize the use of staff.
- Should work to improve ability to be well organized and prepared for any eventuality.

Unsatisfactory

- Does not handle emergencies or unexpected circumstances well.
- Fails to appropriately manage the organizing of projects and workload.
- Fails to keep abreast of staffing needs and changes.
- Has demonstrated poor organizational skills.
- Has not demonstrated an ability to be well organized and prepared for any eventuality.
- Has not shown ability to determine staffing needs accurately.
- Has shown inadequate performance in reorganization efforts.
- Keeps a cluttered desk and conveys a confusing impression.

Productivity

Key Verbs

enhances
exceeds

Key Nouns

contribution	expectations	productivity
effectiveness	output	

Meets or Exceeds

- Can be counted upon to meet or exceed expectations consistently.
- Consistently completes work ahead of schedule.
- Consistently delivers more output than expected.
- Conveys an attitude of dependability and cooperation.
- Enhances the productivity of the entire organization.
- Exceeds expectations in quality and quantity of work.
- Is a highly productive employee.
- Makes a significant contribution to the productivity and effectiveness of the organization.
- Motivation is high, resulting in high output.
- Quality and quantity of work is consistently high.
- Will go beyond job description when appropriate to help out in extraordinary situations.
- Works well with other individuals and departments to enhance the productivity of the entire organization.

Needs Improvement

- Delivers average or barely adequate levels of productivity.
- High level of motivation is not matched by output.
- Is too quick to exclude actions and responsibilities and leave them to others to perform.
- Needs to improve the quality and quantity of work produced.

- Should seek to improve productivity.
- Should strive to better work with other individuals and departments to enhance the productivity of the entire organization.
- Should strive to exceed expectations in quality and quantity of work.
- Should strive to meet or exceed expectations.
- Should work to contribute to productivity gains for the entire organization.
- Should work to make a significant contribution to the overall productivity and effectiveness of the organization.

Unsatisfactory

- Consistently delivers less finished work than expected.
- Consistently fails to meet expectations.
- Conveys a negative attitude about job and company.
- Does not contribute to productivity gains of the entire organization.
- Does not meet expectations in quality and quantity of work.
- Fails to complete work on schedule.
- Fails to work well with other individuals and departments to enhance the productivity of the entire organization.
- Has not demonstrated capability for adequate level of output.
- Productivity is below standards.
- Productivity level is unacceptably low.
- Quality of work is below standards.

Sales Management

Key Verbs

demonstrates
develops
displays
manages

Key Nouns

channels	opportunities	sales goals
distributors	remote offices	sales tools
Internet	representatives	strategies
loyalty	research	training
marketplace		

Meets or Exceeds

- Consistently meets or exceeds sales goals.
- Demonstrates a strong understanding of the role of alternate sales channels.
- Demonstrates ability to adapt well to changes in the marketplace and unexpected conditions.
- Demonstrates ability to manage and motivate sales staff working in remote offices.
- Demonstrates ability to retain major customers in competitive markets.
- Demonstrates strong ability to capitalize on market research.
- Demonstrates superior skills in recruiting and training sales staff.

- Develops and maintains effective sales training programs for supervised staff.
- Develops and manages effective Internet sales strategies.
- Effectively develops new markets.
- Generates strong loyalty from sales staff.
- Has expanded the organization's presence through the effective use of the Internet.
- Is creative in developing opportunities and strategies to enhance goals.
- Keeps marketing department aware of suggestions and requests by customers.
- Makes excellent use of available sales training and sales tools.
- Manages an effective sales incentive program.
- Manages sales staff in remote offices well.
- Motivates and retains successful sales personnel.
- Projects an image of trust and competence.
- Seeks specialized training to improve sales performance.
- Successfully manages independent sales representatives.
- Works closely with marketing department to maintain awareness of new products.
- Works closely with Web developers in creation of online sales presence.
- Works diligently to establish relationships in community that help meet goals.
- Works to retain successful sales staff.
- Works well with other individuals and departments to accomplish sales goals.
- Works well with sales distributors and other indirect channels to expand reach of sales force.

- Works with management to set prices that will maximize sales.
- Works with marketing department to promote new products and services.

Needs Improvement

- Must demonstrate better ability to adapt to changes in the marketplace and unexpected conditions.
- Must do better at retaining successful sales staff.
- Must improve ability to work with sales distributors and other indirect channels to expand reach of sales force.
- Needs to become better at managing independent sales representatives.
- Needs to become more involved with management to set prices that will maximize sales.
- Needs to better demonstrate understanding of the role of alternate sales channels.
- Needs to better motivate and retain successful sales personnel.
- Needs to better understand the importance of being involved in the community as a tool for generating business.
- Needs to devote effort to developing and managing effective Internet sales strategies.
- Needs to display ability to retain major customers in competitive markets.
- Needs to improve ability to manage and motivate sales staff working in remote offices.
- Needs to improve ability to manage sales staff in remote offices.
- Needs to make better use of available market research.

- Needs to make better use of available sales training and sales tools.
- Needs to make effective use of the Internet to expand the organization's presence.
- Needs to more consistently meet or exceed sales goals.
- Needs to work more closely with marketing department to maintain awareness of new products.
- Needs to work more closely with Web developers in creation of online sales presence.
- Needs to work to develop new strategies and opportunities for meeting goals.
- Needs to work to establish a more trustworthy and capable image.
- Should better inform marketing department of suggestions and requests by customers.
- Should strive to become effective in the development of new markets.
- Should strive to develop and maintain effective sales training programs for supervised staff.
- Should strive to establish and maintain an effective sales incentive program.
- Should strive to generate more loyalty from the sales staff.
- Should strive to show higher level of skill in recruiting and training sales staff.
- Should strive to work better with other individuals and departments to accomplish sales goals.
- Should take advantage of available specialized training to improve sales performance.
- Should work with marketing department to promote new products and services.

Unsatisfactory

- Consistently fails to meet sales goals.
- Does not work well with sales distributors and other indirect channels to expand reach of sales force.
- Consistently fails to meet or exceed sales goals.
- Fails to develop relationships with community or business leaders.
- Fails to keep marketing department informed of suggestions and requests by customers.
- Fails to make effective use of the Internet to expand the organization's presence.
- Fails to make good use of available market research.
- Fails to make use of available sales training and sales tools.
- Fails to take advantage of available specialized training to improve sales performance.
- Fails to work closely with marketing department to maintain awareness of new products.
- Has failed to develop and manage effective Internet sales strategies adequately.
- Has failed to manage sales staff in remote offices adequately.
- Has failed to motivate and retain successful sales personnel adequately.
- Has failed to develop and maintain effective sales training programs for supervised staff.
- Has failed to display ability to retain major customers in competitive markets.
- Has failed to establish and maintain an effective sales incentive program.

- Has failed to gain the loyalty of the sales staff.
- Has failed to recruit and train sales staff successfully.
- Has failed to work closely with Web developers in creation of online sales presence.
- Has not demonstrated ability to retain successful sales staff.
- Has not demonstrated ability to work with management to set prices that will maximize sales.
- Has not demonstrated ability to work with marketing department to promote new products and services.
- Has not made effective use of alternate sales channels.
- Has not shown ability to adapt to changes in the marketplace and unexpected conditions.
- Has not shown ability to supervise independent sales representatives adequately.
- Has not shown ability to work well with other individuals and departments to accomplish sales goals.
- Has proved ineffective in the development of new markets.
- Has shown lack of success in the management and motivation of sales staff working in remote offices.
- Is ineffective in developing new strategies or inspiring others to do so.
- Is not considered trustworthy or capable by coworkers.

Supervisory Skills

Key Verbs

demonstrates	maintains	produces
encourages	motivates	seeks

Key Nouns

attendance   policies   support
attitude   promotion   technology
discipline   recognition   tools
guidelines   regulation   training
job description   reinforcement

Meets or Exceeds

- Assists employees in understanding and fulfilling job descriptions.
- Closely follows employee guidelines and regulations set by the company.
- Delivers appropriate recognition and reward to exceptional staffers.
- Demonstrates ability to make the most efficient use of available staff and resources.
- Demonstrates appropriate empathy, consideration, and concern for staff's personal lives.
- Demonstrates considerable skill in supervision and leadership.
- Demonstrates excellent support for new employees.
- Demonstrates exceptional ability at recruiting, hiring, and retaining valuable employees.
- Demonstrates fair and consistent management of employees.
- Demonstrates knowledge of what is involved in getting a job done and is able to convey that message.
- Develops and maintains an effective training program for new employees.

- Displays excellent ability to recognize skills of supervised staff and encourage their appropriate use in the workplace.
- Effectively and clearly communicates guidelines and policies to supervised staff.
- Effectively counsels employees with difficulty meeting policies on attendance and hours.
- Encourages career advancement and personal growth of staff.
- Encourages staff to convey positive attitude.
- Encourages suggestions and new ideas from supervised staff.
- Encourages supervised staff to seek career advancement.
- Establishes and maintains a friendly and respectful work environment.
- Follows organizational guidelines requiring involvement of human resources department in any disciplinary action or dismissal proceeding.
- Gains above-average productivity from staff and resources.
- Gives appropriate positive reinforcement to supervised staff.
- Gives clear and direct instructions to supervised staff.
- Handles difficult employees with skill.
- Has shown excellent skills in supervising temporary and short-term contract staff.
- Is able to maintain a dialogue with staff and encourages the same between coworkers.
- Keeps current on legislative changes and government regulations related to the job.
- Maintains accurate records on attendance and hours.
- Maintains an open-door environment, encouraging interaction with supervised staff.

- Maintains proper documentation of employee actions related to pending disciplinary actions.
- Makes constructive suggestions for improvements in performance and productivity.
- Makes excellent use of available staff and resources.
- Makes realistic demands on supervised staff.
- Makes the most effective use of available technology, tools, and staff.
- Manages personnel matters professionally and equitably.
- Motivates staff through effective use of employee evaluations.
- Motivates supervised staff to be productive and effective in achievement of assignments.
- Moves quickly to deal with unexpected problems.
- Offers effective ongoing coaching and training for supervised staff.
- Produces work schedules that make the most effective use of staff.
- Properly applies company rules for attendance and hours.
- Properly handles misbehavior by supervised staff.
- Seeks high levels of performance and productivity from supervised staff.
- Understands the importance of encouraging high self-esteem in staff.
- Works closely with human resources department to handle significant problems with supervised staff.

Needs Improvement

- Has not consistently followed organizational guidelines requiring involvement of human resources department in any disciplinary action or dismissal proceeding.

- Must better understand tasks assigned to supervised staff.
- Must closely follow employee guidelines and regulations set by the company.
- Must learn to work closely with human resources department to handle significant problems with supervised staff.
- Must maintain proper documentation of employee actions related to pending disciplinary actions.
- Must properly apply company rules for attendance and hours.
- Needs to be more consistent in treatment and management of employees.
- Needs to be more realistic in demands made of supervised staff.
- Needs to better assist employees in understanding and fulfilling job descriptions.
- Needs to better demonstrate appropriate empathy, consideration, and concern for staff's personal lives.
- Needs to better motivate supervised staff to be productive and effective in achievement of assignments.
- Needs to develop and maintain an effective training program for new employees.
- Needs to counsel employees with difficulty meeting policies on attendance and hours effectively.
- Needs to give clear and direct instructions to supervised staff.
- Needs to improve ability to schedule staff for the most productivity.
- Needs to improve impressions and perceptions conveyed to coworkers.
- Needs to improve skills as a supervisor.
- Needs to improve skills in supervising temporary and short-term contract staff.

- Needs to improve use of available technology, tools, and staff.
- Needs to improve management of personnel matters to be more professional and equitable.
- Needs to keep current on legislative changes and government regulations related to the job.
- Needs to learn new skills to properly handle misbehavior by supervised staff.
- Needs to learn to better handle difficult employees.
- Needs to maintain accurate records on attendance and hours.
- Needs to make better use of available staff and resources.
- Needs to make better use of employee evaluations to motivate staff.
- Needs to react more quickly to unexpected problems.
- Needs to work to recognize skills of supervised staff and encourage their appropriate use in the workplace.
- Should be more consistent in delivering appropriate recognition and reward to exceptional staffers.
- Should encourage supervised staff to make suggestions and offer new ideas.
- Should encourage supervised staff to seek career advancement.
- Should give appropriate positive reinforcement to supervised staff.
- Should improve ability to communicate guidelines and policies to supervised staff effectively and clearly.
- Should offer constructive suggestions for improvements in performance and productivity.
- Should offer effective ongoing coaching and training for supervised staff.

- Should seek high levels of performance and productivity from supervised staff.
- Should seek to improve productivity from staff and resources.
- Should strive to encourage more interaction with supervised staff.
- Should work to encourage career advancement and personal growth of staff.
- Should work to establish a more friendly and respectful work environment.
- Should work to improve ability to recruit, hire, and retain valuable employees.

Unsatisfactory

- Demonstrates a lack of understanding of instructions to staffers.
- Develops inefficient work schedules that reduce productivity.
- Discourages supervised staff from making suggestions and offering new ideas.
- Does not demonstrate appropriate empathy, consideration, and concern for staff's personal lives.
- Does not effectively and clearly communicate guidelines and policies to supervised staff.
- Does not encourage a friendly and respectful work environment.
- Does not encourage career advancement and personal growth of staff.
- Does not give appropriate positive reinforcement to supervised staff.

- Does not maintain accurate records on attendance and hours.
- Does not make effective use of employee evaluations to motivate staff.
- Does not make good use of available staff and resources.
- Does not manage personnel matters in a professional or equitable manner.
- Does not offer encouragement to supervised staff to seek career advancement.
- Does not push staff to high levels of performance and productivity.
- Does not show skill in recruiting, hiring, and retaining valuable employees.
- Fails to handle difficult employees adequately.
- Fails to supervise temporary and short-term contract staff adequately.
- Fails to assist employees in understanding and fulfilling job descriptions.
- Fails to follow employee guidelines and regulations set by the company closely.
- Fails to gain acceptable productivity from staff and resources.
- Fails to give clear and direct instructions to supervised staff.
- Fails to keep current on legislative changes and government regulations related to the job.
- Fails to maintain proper documentation of employee actions related to pending disciplinary actions.
- Fails to offer constructive suggestions for improvements in performance and productivity.

- Fails to apply company rules for attendance and hours properly.
- Fails to handle misbehavior by supervised staff properly.
- Fails to react rapidly to unexpected problems.
- Fails to work closely with human resources department to handle significant problems with supervised staff.
- Has failed to develop and maintain an effective training program for new employees.
- Has failed to counsel employees with difficulty meeting policies on attendance and hours effectively.
- Has failed to follow organizational guidelines requiring involvement of human resources department in any disciplinary action or dismissal proceeding.
- Has failed to make effective use of available technology, tools, and staff.
- Has failed to offer effective ongoing coaching and training for supervised staff.
- Has not demonstrated consistent ability to motivate supervised staff to be productive and effective in achievement of assignments.
- Has not demonstrated ability to recognize skills of supervised staff and encourage their appropriate use in the workplace.
- Has not demonstrated acceptable skills as a supervisor and leader.
- Is inconsistent in delivering appropriate recognition and reward to exceptional staffers.
- Is inconsistent in treatment and management of employees.
- Is inefficient in allocation of available staff and resources.

- Is unable to display flexibility in dealing with different personalities.
- Makes a poor impression on coworkers.
- Makes unrealistic demands of supervised staff.
- Remains remote from staff, discouraging interaction.

Training and Employee Development Skills

Key Verbs

demonstrates	displays	seeks
develops	manages	

Key Nouns

advancement	Internet	professional development
counseling	orientation	seminars
development	potential	training

Meets or Exceeds

- Demonstrates skill in identifying employees with potential for advancement.
- Consistently seeks to broaden base of experience and knowledge to advance career.
- Demonstrates ability to recognize employees who could benefit from training.
- Demonstrates exceptional interest in professional development of supervised staff.
- Demonstrates long-range plan for personal and professional advancement.
- Demonstrates notable skills in establishing professional development programs.

- Demonstrates through actions the importance of advanced training.
- Develops effective career advancement programs.
- Develops succession strategies for key staffers.
- Devotes great attention to the professional development needs of supervised staff.
- Encourages enterprisewide professional development programs.
- Encourages supervised staff to make use of professional development programs for advancement.
- Encourages supervised staff to seek out advancement opportunities.
- Fosters an environment of positive reinforcement.
- Has a proven track record of finding staff with underutilized potential and guiding them to professional development programs.
- Helps management develop career advancement programs.
- Maintains an "open door policy" in dealing with employees on every level.
- Maintains backup plans for replacement of key staffers when needed.
- Makes full use of available training tools, including seminars, software-based training, and the Internet.
- Manages new employee orientation with great skill.
- Recognized as a career counselor and coach.
- Seeks out and makes use of professional development programs to further career.
- Shows exceptional abilities in helping struggling employees to find appropriate training and assistance.

- Shows great skill in determining needs for staff development.
- Shows great skill in discovering employees with untapped potential.
- Takes a hands-on approach to training.
- Takes every opportunity to advance career through professional development programs.

Needs Improvement

- Should work to identify staffers with advancement potential.
- Needs to assist management in the development of career advancement programs.
- Needs to be more accessible to employees.
- Needs to develop succession strategies for key staffers.
- Needs to devote more attention to determining needs for staff development.
- Needs to devote more attention to professional development needs of supervised staff.
- Needs to establish and maintain backup plans for replacement of key staffers when needed.
- Needs to foster an environment of positive reinforcement.
- Needs to recognize employees who could benefit from training.
- Should demonstrate through actions the importance of advanced training.
- Should develop a long-range plan for personal and professional advancement.
- Should devote more attention to professional development of supervised staff.
- Should encourage creation of an enterprisewide professional development program.

- Should encourage supervised staff to make use of professional development programs for advancement.
- Should encourage supervised staff to seek out advancement opportunities.
- Should improve skills in giving new employee orientation.
- Should make better use of available professional development programs to further career.
- Should make better use of available training tools, including seminars, software-based training, and the Internet.
- Should seek to discover employees with untapped potential.
- Should seek ways to help struggling employees find appropriate training and assistance.
- Should work to broaden base of experience and knowledge to advance career.
- Takes a hands-off approach to training.

Unsatisfactory

- Does not seek to find employees with potential for advancement.
- Does not adequately prepare new employees at orientation session.
- Fails to devote attention to determining needs for staff development.
- Fails to encourage supervised staff to seek out advancement opportunities.
- Fails to foster an environment of positive reinforcement.
- Fails to make good use of available training tools, including seminars, software-based training, and the Internet.

- Has failed to assist management in the development of career advancement programs.
- Has failed to determine professional development needs of supervised staff.
- Has failed to encourage supervised staff to make use of professional development programs for advancement.
- Has failed to establish and maintain backup plans for replacement of key staffers when needed.
- Has not broadened base of experience and knowledge beyond current specialty.
- Has not demonstrated capability of teaching or offering guidance to coworkers.
- Has not made use of available professional development programs to further career.
- Has not shown ability to develop effective professional development programs.
- Has proved unable to establish meaningful connection with employees.
- Ignores the needs of struggling employees.
- Makes no effort to seek out employees who could benefit from training.

Chapter 8

PERSONALITY AND HUMAN RELATIONS

POLITICOS HAVE AN ALL-PURPOSE DODGE: "Don't blame you; don't blame me. Blame that fellow behind the tree."

That doesn't work in an office setting, but that doesn't prevent staffers from trying. The blame game is a common pursuit, as are interpersonal conflicts, character flaws, and meltdowns under stress.

As with other qualitative attributes, be sure to focus on the performance and the individual. A worker who displays a less-than-perfect temperament may nevertheless be highly productive or otherwise capable.

- Accountability
- Cooperation and teamwork skills
- Interpersonal/human relations skills
- Personal maturity and tact
- Personal potential
- Personality, character, and temperament

Accountability

Key Verbs

accepts
demonstrates
handles

Key Nouns

accountability	appropriateness	guidance
acknowledgment	assignments	responsibility
actions	decisions	tasks

Meets or Exceeds

- Accepts responsibility for all actions, decisions, and tasks delegated to subordinates.
- Can be depended upon to act professionally and appropriately in any situation.
- Clearly accepts liability for errors when appropriate.
- Demonstrates ability to acknowledge mistakes and learn from them.
- Handles criticism well, admits mistakes, and makes corrections quickly and willingly.
- Is open to suggestions and guidance.
- Is willing to share success and accept the responsibility of failure of a project.

Needs Improvement

- Is not open to suggestions and guidance.
- Must learn to act professionally and appropriately in any situation.

- Must learn to handle criticism well and admit mistakes.
- Not always willing to accept liability for errors.
- Needs to accept responsibility for all actions, decisions, and tasks delegated to subordinates.
- Needs to learn to share success and accept responsibility for failure of a project.
- Should make corrections quickly and willingly.

Unsatisfactory

- Does not accept responsibility for all actions, decisions, and tasks delegated to subordinates.
- Cannot be counted upon to act professionally and appropriately in any situation.
- Does not handle criticism well and admit mistakes.
- Fails to make corrections quickly and willingly.
- Is not open to suggestions and guidance.
- Is unwilling to accept blame for failure.
- Is unwilling to give credit to subordinates or accept any part of failure of a project.

Cooperation and Teamwork Skills

Key Verbs

cooperates	encourages	promotes
coordinates	gives	selects
demonstrates	meets or exceeds	shares

Key Nouns

cooperation	resources	teamwork
goals	team player	

Meets or Exceeds

- Brings together coworkers for effective teamwork.
- Champions teamwork and cooperation throughout the enterprise.
- Demonstrates ability to develop and supervise effective teams.
- Effectively coordinates multiple work teams to achieve organizational goals.
- Encourages cooperative efforts.
- Gives clear and precise instructions and guidelines to teams.
- Has made department a model for teamwork and cooperation.
- Helps bring together previously uncooperative individuals and groups for team efforts.
- Is a proven team player.
- Is willing to be a team worker rather than a manager if it is essential to the success of a project.
- Makes the best use of available resources and staff in managing teams.
- Organizes effective workgroups and teams.
- Promotes cooperation throughout the organization.
- Promotes cooperative efforts.
- Promotes teamwork and cooperation.
- Selects highly qualified leaders and members of work teams.
- Works well with multiple teams and departments.

Needs Improvement

- Must better coordinate multiple work teams to achieve organizational goals.
- Must deliver clear and precise instructions and guidelines to teams.
- Must display ability to work well with multiple teams and departments.
- Must learn to make the best use of available resources and staff in managing teams.
- Needs to be more available to coworkers when necessary for the success of a project.
- Needs to bring together coworkers for effective teamwork.
- Needs to demonstrate ability to develop and supervise effective teams.
- Needs to improve ability to work together in cooperative efforts.
- Needs to organize effective workgroups and teams.
- Needs to show better ability to select highly qualified leaders and members of work teams.
- Needs to work to bring together previously uncooperative individuals and groups for team efforts.
- Seems more comfortable working solo.
- Should champion team efforts.
- Should encourage more cooperation in the department and throughout the organization.
- Should promote cooperative efforts.
- Should work to improve departmental teamwork and cooperation.
- Should work to promote cooperation throughout the organization.

Unsatisfactory

- Appears to be incapable of working as part of a group.
- Does not give clear and precise instructions and guidelines to teams.
- Does not work well with multiple teams and departments.
- Does not work well with others in cooperative efforts.
- Fails to demonstrate ability to develop and supervise effective teams.
- Fails to make the best use of available resources and staff in managing teams.
- Fails to promote cooperative or team efforts in the enterprise.
- Has consistently been aloof and unapproachable when dealing with employees.
- Has failed to bring together coworkers for effective teamwork.
- Has failed to bring together uncooperative individuals and groups for team efforts.
- Has failed to encourage more cooperation in the department and throughout the organization.
- Has made no significant effort to improve departmental teamwork and cooperation.
- Has not demonstrated ability to effectively coordinate multiple work teams to achieve organizational goals.
- Has not promoted cooperation throughout the organization.
- Has not shown ability to select highly qualified leaders and members of work teams.
- Has resisted efforts to improve teamwork and cooperation.

Interpersonal/Human Relations Skills

Key Verbs

builds	displays	respects
conveys	encourages	shows
demonstrates	promotes	understands
develops	recognizes	

Key Nouns

acceptance	honesty	respect
beliefs	rapport	sincerity
confrontations	relationships	values
consensus	reliability	workgroups
diversity		

Meets or Exceeds

- Appreciates the importance of diversity and conveys that feeling to others.
- Avoids unnecessary or inappropriate confrontations.
- Brings together and maintains effective workgroups.
- Builds an environment of trust.
- Builds close relationships with coworkers.
- Conveys empathy for the needs of others.
- Demonstrates a willingness to help others.
- Demonstrates ability to get along with others.
- Demonstrates ability to help others get along and work together.
- Demonstrates reliability and honesty in establishing relationships.

- Demonstrates sincere care for others.
- Establishes rapport with coworkers.
- Has earned the respect of others.
- Helps build consensus among coworkers.
- Helps build trust among coworkers.
- Is an effective and well-respected manager.
- Is well accepted by others.
- Knows how to get along with coworkers.
- Makes a good first impression in every situation.
- Promotes positive relationships among staffers.
- Promotes respect among coworkers.
- Recognizes and accepts others.
- Respects the opinions and beliefs of others.
- Shows a good understanding of human behavior.
- Shows appropriate respect for coworkers and customers of different backgrounds, cultures, and religions.
- Understands and respects the values and beliefs of others.
- Works hard to be politically correct.
- Works to gain acceptance by others.
- Works well with multiple supervisors or superiors.
- Works well with others.

Needs Improvement

- Must establish better rapport with coworkers.
- Must improve skills to become an effective and well-respected manager.
- Needs to build an environment of trust.
- Needs to build close relationships with coworkers.
- Needs to demonstrate a better ability to get along with others.

- Needs to demonstrate a good understanding of human behavior.
- Needs to demonstrate a willingness to help others.
- Needs to demonstrate reliability and honesty in establishing relationships.
- Needs to demonstrate sincere care for others.
- Needs to gain acceptance by others.
- Needs to help build consensus among coworkers.
- Needs to learn how to get along with coworkers.
- Needs to learn how to work well with multiple supervisors or superiors.
- Needs to learn to bring together and maintain effective workgroups.
- Needs to promote positive relationships among staffers.
- Needs to recognize and accept others.
- Needs to work better with others.
- Should better convey empathy for the needs of others.
- Should demonstrate respect for the opinions and beliefs of others.
- Should find ways to make a good first impression in every situation.
- Should promote respect among coworkers.
- Should seek to be better accepted by others.
- Should work to avoid unnecessary or inappropriate confrontations.
- Should work to build trust among coworkers.
- Should work to develop and show appropriate respect for coworkers and customers of different backgrounds, cultures, and religions.
- Should work to earn the respect of others.

- Should work to understand and respect the values and beliefs of others.
- Sometimes makes judgments based on stereotypes.
- Tends to introduce inappropriate comments or language.

Unsatisfactory

- Appears biased and inflexible.
- Could not demonstrate sincere care for others.
- Could not work well with multiple supervisors or superiors.
- Does not show appropriate respect for coworkers and customers of different backgrounds, cultures, and religions.
- Does not work well with others.
- Fails to establish good rapport with coworkers.
- Is ineffective as a manager.
- Is not respected as a manager.
- Often uses inappropriate or offensive language.
- Refuses to attempt to understand and respect the values and beliefs of others.
- Refuses to show respect for the opinions and beliefs of others.
- Unable to avoid unnecessary or inappropriate confrontations.
- Unable to build close relationships with coworkers.
- Unable to build consensus among coworkers.
- Unable to convey empathy for the needs of others.
- Unable to demonstrate a willingness to help others.
- Unable to demonstrate an understanding of human behavior.
- Unable to demonstrate reliability and honesty in establishing relationships.

- Unable to earn the respect of others.
- Unable to establish an environment of trust.
- Unable to find ways to make a good first impression in every situation.
- Unable to gain acceptance by others.
- Unable to get along with others.
- Unable to learn to bring together and maintain effective workgroups.
- Unable to promote positive relationships among staffers.
- Unable to promote respect among coworkers.
- Unable to seek better acceptance by others.
- Unwilling to build trust among coworkers.
- Unwilling to learn how to get along with coworkers.
- Unwilling to recognize and accept others.

Personal Maturity and Tact

Key Verbs

avoids	displays	responds
controls	manages	shows
demonstrates		

Key Nouns

appropriateness	emotions	professionalism
calm	equanimity	responsibility
control	guidelines	tact
demeanor	judgment	understanding
diplomacy	maturity	

Meets or Exceeds

- Accepts responsibility for actions and those of supervised staff.
- Assists others in coping with difficult situations and challenges.
- Avoids arguments and confrontations wherever possible.
- Controls difficult situations with maturity and equanimity.
- Demonstrates diplomacy and tact in dealing with supervised staff and clients.
- Demonstrates maturity and understanding in actions.
- Demonstrates self-control in all situations.
- Demonstrates understanding and adherence to personal behavior guidelines of employee manual.
- Displays maturity and professionalism in all situations.
- Displays maturity in decision-making and management.
- Does not allow emotion to interfere with decision-making.
- Follows guidelines for personal responsibility and behavior included in employee handbook.
- Has taken advantage of available training to help manage difficult situations and individuals.
- Is a model of diplomacy and good judgment.
- Is able to diffuse volatile situations at an early stage.
- Is able to exert a calming influence over others.
- Is consistently polite and well mannered.
- Is polite and tactful in difficult situations.
- Is willing to admit errors and seek new solutions.
- Keeps anger and emotions under control.
- Manages confrontations with maturity and professionalism.
- Responds appropriately to provocation by staff or clients.

- Shows a calm and controlled demeanor.
- Works well with other individuals and departments to manage difficult situations.

Needs Improvement

- Is often lax in judgment and diplomacy.
- Must accept responsibility for actions and those of supervised staff.
- Must demonstrate understanding and adherence to personal behavior guidelines of employee manual.
- Must follow guidelines for personal responsibility and behavior included in employee handbook.
- Must learn to better work with other individuals and departments to manage difficult situations.
- Must respond appropriately to provocation by staff or clients.
- Needs to be consistently polite and well mannered.
- Needs to be polite and tactful in difficult situations.
- Needs to be willing to admit errors and seek new solutions.
- Needs to better control anger and emotions.
- Needs to better demonstrate maturity and understanding in actions.
- Needs to demonstrate more diplomacy and tact in dealing with supervised staff and clients.
- Needs to display more maturity and professionalism.
- Needs to learn to manage confrontations with maturity and professionalism.
- Needs to show more maturity in decision-making and management.

- Needs to strive to avoid arguments and confrontations wherever possible.
- Needs to take advantage of available training to help manage difficult situations and individuals.
- Should assist others in coping with difficult situations and challenges.
- Should strive to prevent emotions from interfering with decision-making.
- Should strive to show a calm and controlled demeanor.
- Should work to improve control of emotions in difficult situations.

Unsatisfactory

- Allows emotions to interfere with decision-making.
- Demonstrates an unwillingness to admit errors.
- Does not demonstrate diplomacy and tact in dealing with supervised staff and clients.
- Does not display maturity in actions.
- Does not maintain self-control in all situations.
- Does not respond appropriately to provocation by staff or clients.
- Fails to accept responsibility for actions and those of supervised staff.
- Fails to assist others in coping with difficult situations and challenges.
- Fails to demonstrate maturity in decision-making and management.
- Fails to demonstrate understanding and adherence to personal behavior guidelines of employee manual.
- Fails to keep anger and emotions under control.

- Fails to manage confrontation with maturity and professionalism.
- Fails to take advantage of available training to help manage difficult situations and individuals.
- Has demonstrated lack of ability to work well with other individuals and departments to manage difficult situations.
- Has demonstrated loss of emotional control in difficult situations.
- Has not shown ability to avoid arguments and confrontations.
- Is not always polite and tactful in difficult situations.
- Is not consistently polite and well mannered.
- Often displays poor judgment and a lack of diplomatic skills.
- Uses inappropriate language for workplace.
- Violates guidelines for personal responsibility and behavior included in employee handbook.

Personal Potential

Key Verbs

demonstrates
displays
seeks
shows

Key Nouns

advancement
potential
promotion
responsibility

Meets or Exceeds

- Demonstrates capability to assume more job responsibility.
- Demonstrates commitment to advancement through pursuit of training and advanced education.
- Demonstrates leadership ability.
- Demonstrates management potential.
- Demonstrates obvious qualifications for advancement.
- Displays tremendous potential for advancement.
- Displays willingness to accept new responsibilities and tasks.
- Is capable of assuming new job tasks and assignments.
- Is willing to go above and beyond job description to ensure success of a project.
- Seeks training and advanced education to improve skills.
- Should be considered for appropriate advancement.
- Should be considered for leadership position.
- Should be considered for management position.
- Shows great potential for advancement.
- Someone we don't want to lose.

Needs Improvement

- Needs to be willing to go beyond job description to ensure success of project.
- Needs to demonstrate potential for advancement.
- Needs to demonstrate qualifications for management position.
- Potential not yet fully realized.
- Should be more willing to accept new responsibilities and tasks.
- Should better demonstrate management potential.

- Should demonstrate capability to assume more job responsibility.
- Should demonstrate commitment to advancement through pursuit of training and advanced education.
- Should seek training and advanced education to improve skills.
- Should strive to better demonstrate leadership ability.
- Should strive to demonstrate capability of assuming new job tasks and assignments.
- Should work to better demonstrate qualifications for advancement.

Unsatisfactory

- Does not demonstrate qualifications for advancement.
- Does not display potential for advancement.
- Fails to demonstrate leadership ability.
- Has failed to demonstrate capability to assume more job responsibility.
- Has not demonstrated commitment to advancement through pursuit of training and advanced education.
- Has not demonstrated management potential.
- Has not demonstrated the likelihood of having a future in this organization.
- Has not shown capability to assume new job tasks and assignments.
- Has not sought training and advanced education to improve skills.
- Is unwilling to accept a challenge or do more than the minimum.
- Resists accepting new responsibilities and tasks.

Personality, Character, and Temperament

Key Verbs

demonstrates
displays
projects
shows

Key Nouns

calm	forthrightness	polish
character	honesty	popularity
courtesy	objectivity	presence
disposition	personality	professionalism
enthusiasm	poise	temperament

Meets or Exceeds

- Is a reliable, calm presence.
- Is a well-respected and liked staffer.
- Is calm, cool, and collected.
- Is cheerful and pleasant in disposition.
- Consistently demonstrates strong moral character and honesty.
- Is courteous and professional.
- Demonstrates considerable poise in all situations.
- Demonstrates great sincerity and warmth.
- Demonstrates appropriate use of humor in the workplace.
- Has a professional and courteous attitude toward customers.
- Is honest and forthright in all relations.
- Is not afraid to be a role model.
- Is pleasant and easy to work with.

- Is polite and respectful in all dealings.
- Is popular with coworkers for abilities and attitude toward others.
- Is professional and businesslike in relations with staff and clients.
- Projects enthusiasm and energy in all efforts.
- Is respected for honesty and objectivity in all dealings.
- Is very polished.

Needs Improvement

- Could be more honest and forthright.
- Does not project an open and accepting personality.
- Is not always cheerful and pleasant to others.
- Must find ways to interact in a professional and courteous manner with coworkers.
- Needs to improve professional and businesslike demeanor in relations with staff and clients.
- Needs to learn to treat customers in a professional and courteous manner.
- Needs to modify temperament to be more approachable.
- Should readily accept responsibility for new projects or assignments.
- Should strive for a greater degree of honesty and objectivity in all dealings.
- Should work on displaying a calmer presence.
- Should work to be more courteous and professional.
- Should work to become more polished in relations with others.
- Should work to display appropriate humor in the workplace.
- Should work to project more enthusiasm in job tasks.

Unsatisfactory

- Does not interact in a professional and courteous manner with coworkers.
- Does not readily accept responsibility for new projects or assignments.
- Does not treat customers in a professional and courteous manner.
- Has been less than professional and businesslike in relations with staff and clients.
- Has demonstrated a lack of honesty and objectivity in dealings with others.
- Has demonstrated an inappropriate use of humor in the workplace.
- Has demonstrated lack of courtesy in the workplace.
- Has offended others with inappropriate use of humor.
- Has proved to be less than honest and forthright in relations with others.
- Has shown lack of professionalism in relations with others.
- Is often unpleasant in dealings with others.
- Is seen as unapproachable and standoffish.
- Lacks enthusiasm in performance of job assignments.
- Lacks polish in relations with others.
- Loses self-control in many situations.
- Often displays a condescending and mean-spirited attitude.

Chapter 9

PROFESSIONAL SKILLS

THE MODERN WORKPLACE includes some very specialized professionals who sometimes seem to speak an alien language, manipulating mysterious numbers or operating machines that do something very meaningful—or so you are told.

You've got to know the territory when it comes time to evaluate a professional: information technology, accounting, government relations, human resources, and other such posts.

- Accounting and payroll officers
- Computer services manager
- Executive secretary
- Government relations manager
- Human resources manager
- In-house training staff
- In-house travel coordinator
- Legal services personnel
- Mailroom supervisor
- Maintenance and janitorial
- Marketing director
- Meeting planner
- Public relations/public information
- Purchasing agent

- Receptionist
- Security officer
- Warehouse/stockroom staff

Accounting and Payroll Officers

Key Verbs

assists	displays	negotiates
demonstrates	monitors	reduces

Key Nouns

accounting	budgets	expenditures
accounts payable	credit services	payroll services
accounts receivable		

Meets or Exceeds

- Assists departments in planning budgets and tracking expenditures.
- Closely follows new regulations and laws affecting accounting procedures.
- Closely monitors accounts payable, establishing and maintaining a schedule that most benefits the organization.
- Demonstrates excellent coordination with benefits manager to keep payroll system current.
- Demonstrates excellent skills in managing accounts receivable, minimizing losses.
- Demonstrates excellent use of available tools and technologies to track accounting and payroll needs.

- Displays excellent understanding of the products and services of the organization.
- Has demonstrated ability to negotiate and keep current an advantageous contract for outside supplier of payroll services.
- Has reduced costs by bringing payroll services in-house.
- Keeps current on new technologies and tools.
- Negotiates advantageous contracts with outside suppliers of accounting, payroll, and credit services.
- Works closely with all departments in developing budgets.
- Works closely with human resources to establish and maintain excellent payroll management system.
- Works closely with sales and marketing departments to set credit terms for customers.
- Works well with outside auditors in preparation of financial statements and compliance reports.

Needs Improvement

- Does not display deep understanding of the products and services of the organization.
- Must improve relations with outside auditors in preparation of financial statements and compliance reports.
- Must keep more current on new technologies and tools.
- Must more closely follow new regulations and laws affecting accounting procedures.
- Needs to develop skills to negotiate advantageous contracts with outside suppliers of accounting, payroll, and credit services.
- Needs to improve ability to manage accounts receivable, minimizing losses.

- Needs to improve attention to accounts payable, establishing and maintaining a schedule that most benefits the organization.
- Needs to improve capability to negotiate and keep current an advantageous contract for outside supplier of payroll services.
- Needs to improve cooperation with other departments in planning budgets and tracking expenditures.
- Needs to improve working relationship with human resources department to establish and maintain excellent payroll management system.
- Needs to make better use of available tools and technologies to track accounting and payroll needs.
- Needs to work closer with sales and marketing departments to set credit terms for customers.
- Should improve coordination with benefits manager to keep payroll system current.
- Should strive to reduce costs by bringing payroll services in-house.
- Should work more closely with all departments in developing budgets.

Unsatisfactory

- Does not demonstrate necessary skills to negotiate and keep current an advantageous contract for outside supplier of payroll services.
- Does not make appropriate use of available tools and technologies to track accounting and payroll needs.
- Fails to demonstrate understanding of the products and services of the organization.

- Fails to work closely with human resources department to establish and maintain mission-critical payroll-management system.
- Has been unable or unwilling to work with benefits manager to keep payroll system current.
- Has demonstrated a lack of understanding and adherence to new regulations and laws affecting accounting procedures.
- Has failed to adequately manage accounts payable, establishing and maintaining a schedule that most benefits the organization.
- Has failed to cooperate with other departments in planning budgets and tracking expenditures.
- Has failed to keep current on new technologies and tools.
- Has failed to reduce costs by bringing payroll services in-house, as directed by management.
- Has failed to work closely with sales and marketing departments to set credit terms for customers.
- Has not displayed acceptable skills in managing accounts receivable, minimizing losses.
- Has proved unable or unwilling to work closely with all departments in developing budgets.
- Has proved unable to improve relations with outside auditors in preparation of financial statements and compliance reports.
- Has proved unable to negotiate advantageous contracts with outside suppliers of accounting, payroll, and credit services.

Computer Services Manager

Key Verbs

coordinates	develops	identifies
creates	establishes	negotiates

Key Nouns

computer maintenance	response time	trade shows
e-mail	strategies	upgrade
Internet	support	

Meets or Exceeds

- Created an effective in-house computer support desk available to all users.
- Developed an enterprisewide upgrade program that saved (thousands/millions) of dollars in operating expenses.
- Enforces the organization's policies on inappropriate use of the Internet and e-mail by employees.
- Establishes important contacts at industry functions, trade shows, and conventions.
- Has developed an effective in-house computer maintenance and repair department, reducing costs and improving response time.
- Is able to identify a problem and engage the suitable technician to remedy it.
- Is valued as an in-house expert on computer strategies.
- Keeps staff up-to-date on organization policies regarding inappropriate use of the Internet and e-mail.
- Makes the effort to attend trade shows and seminars to

keep current on computer technologies related to the organization's mission.

- Negotiated a cost-effective contract with an outside firm to maintain and repair computer equipment.
- Represents the organization well at trade shows and conventions.
- Together with in-house training staff, has developed an effective education program to improve employee computer skills.
- Works closely with legal and security departments to safeguard the privacy of personnel files.
- Works closely with other departments to make the most of computer technology to advance sales and research.
- Works well with outside consultants in designing organizational strategies for computer usage.

Needs Improvement

- Must work to keep staff up-to-date on organization policies regarding inappropriate use of the Internet and e-mail.
- Needs to become more familiar with the changing capabilities of hardware and software.
- Needs to better enforce the organization's policies on inappropriate use of the Internet and e-mail by employees.
- Needs to concentrate on making contacts with colleagues in the industry.
- Needs to coordinate efforts with other departments to make the most of computer technology to advance sales and research.
- Needs to improve relations with outside consultants in designing organizational strategies for computer usage.

- Needs to take better advantage of trade shows and conventions to make contacts and research new equipment and procedures.
- Needs to work with in-house training staff to develop an effective education program to improve employee computer skills.
- Should make the effort to attend trade shows and seminars to keep current on computer technologies related to the organization's mission.
- Should seek to create an effective in-house computer support desk available to all users.
- Should strive to negotiate a cost-effective contract with an outside firm to maintain and repair computer equipment.
- Should work to develop an effective in-house computer maintenance and repair department, reducing costs and improving response time.
- Should work to develop an enterprisewide upgrade program to save operating costs through the use of more efficient and capable computers.

Unsatisfactory

- Does not demonstrate understanding or comfort with the use of advanced office machines and software.
- Fails to participate in appropriate trade shows or conventions.
- Has declined to make the effort to attend trade shows and seminars to keep current on computer technologies related to the organization's mission.
- Has failed to develop an effective in-house computer maintenance and repair department, reducing costs and improving response time.

- Has failed to enforce the organization's policies on inappropriate use of the Internet and e-mail by employees.
- Has failed to work with in-house training staff to develop an effective education program to improve employee computer skills.
- Has not demonstrated ability to make contacts with contemporaries within the industry.
- Has not demonstrated ability to work well with outside consultants in designing organizational strategies for computer usage.
- Has not shown ability to work closely with other departments to make the most of computer technology to advance sales and research.
- Has proved unable to create an effective in-house computer support desk available to all users.
- Has proved unable to develop an acceptable enterprisewide upgrade program to save operating costs through the use of more efficient and capable computers.
- Must keep staff up-to-date on organization policies regarding inappropriate use of the Internet and e-mail.
- Was unsuccessful in negotiations for a cost-effective contract with an outside firm to maintain computer equipment.

Executive Secretary

Key Verbs

   demonstrates
   displays
   manages
   presents

Key Nouns

chain of command	decorum	schedule
confidential matters	discretion	trustworthiness

Meets or Exceeds

- Demonstrates a high degree of appropriate discretion and decorum in the executive suite.
- Demonstrates strong familiarity with department heads and chain of command.
- Demonstrates trustworthiness in handling confidential financial and personnel matters.
- Displays an excellent command of technologies and tools.
- Displays strong understanding of the products and services of the enterprise.
- Effectively manages the schedule of executive officers.
- Presents a highly polished, professional appearance.
- Telephone techniques and message-taking skills are excellent.

Needs Improvement

- Does not always communicate professionally on the telephone.
- Does not display strong familiarity with department heads and chain of command.
- Needs to keep current with changes in personnel.
- Must become more effective at managing the schedule of executive officers.
- Must improve telephone techniques and message-taking skills.
- Must work to keep technical skills current.

- Needs to improve ability to demonstrate appropriate discretion and decorum in the executive suite.
- Needs to improve command of technologies and tools.
- Seems uncomfortable in the executive suite.
- Should strive to add greater understanding of the products and services of the enterprise.
- Should work to better demonstrate trustworthiness in handling confidential financial and personnel matters.
- Should work to present a more professional appearance.

Unsatisfactory

- Does not demonstrate appropriate discretion and decorum in the executive suite.
- Does not display sufficient understanding of the products and services of the enterprise and has failed to take appropriate steps to improve ability.
- Does not keep current with changes in personnel.
- Does not keep pace with duties at the executive level.
- Failed to appropriately safeguard the privacy of personnel matters.
- Fails to communicate professionally on the telephone.
- Has demonstrated lack of familiarity with staff and officers of the organization.
- Has failed to demonstrate command of technologies and tools.
- Has failed to demonstrate trustworthiness in handling confidential financial and personnel matters.
- Has failed to display strong familiarity with department heads and chain of command.
- Has failed to keep technical skills current.

- Has not taken the effort to become more effective at managing the schedule of executive officers.
- Has proved unable to improve telephone techniques and message-taking skills to acceptable levels.
- Has proved unable to present a polished, professional appearance at work in keeping with the job description.
- Quality of telephone messages is unacceptable.

Government Relations Manager

Key Verbs

coordinates
maintains
supports
works

Key Nouns

| compliance | laws | regulations |
| federal/state agencies | legislators | task forces |

Meets or Exceeds

- Ably represents the organization's position in meetings with regulators.
- Coordinates government relations work with appropriate departments of the organization, including legal services, human resources, and finance.
- Demonstrates deep understanding of the organization's products and services, and the relationship to state and federal regulators and legislators.

- Keeps current on changes to federal and state regulations and laws, advising appropriate departments in the organization as necessary.
- Maintains close ties to staff of government agencies and state and federal legislators in support of the organization's mission.
- Supports the organization's mission through participation in task forces and commissions.
- Works closely with federal and state agencies to ensure compliance with regulations.

Needs Improvement

- Does not demonstrate deep understanding of the organization's products and services, and the relationship to state and federal regulators and legislators.
- Must establish and maintain close ties to staff of government agencies and state and federal legislators in support of the organization's mission.
- Must find ways to better coordinate government relations work with appropriate departments of the organization, including legal services, human resources, and finance.
- Must work more closely with federal and state agencies to ensure compliance with regulations.
- Needs to improve ability to represent the organization's position in meetings with regulators.
- Needs to keep current on changes to federal and state regulations and laws, advising appropriate departments in the organization as necessary.
- Needs to support the organization's mission through participation in task forces and commissions.

Unsatisfactory

- Does not demonstrate ability to work closely with federal and state agencies to ensure compliance with regulations.
- Fails to demonstrate deep understanding of the organization's products and services, and the relationship to state and federal regulators and legislators.
- Fails to keep current on changes to federal and state regulations and laws, advising appropriate departments in the organization as necessary.
- Fails to find ways to better coordinate government relations work with appropriate departments of the organization, including legal services, human resources, and finance.
- Has not demonstrated ability to represent the organization's position in meetings with regulators.
- Has proved unable or unwilling to support the organization's mission through participation in task forces and commissions.
- Has proved unable to establish and maintain close ties to staff of government agencies and state and federal legislators in support of the organization's mission.

Human Resources Manager

Key Verbs

assists
demonstrates
displays
manages

Key Nouns

orientation	records	regulations
personnel policies	recruiting	rewards
privacy		

Meets or Exceeds

- Assists managers in developing and running employee orientation programs.
- Coordinates personnel policies with in-house counsel.
- Demonstrates an excellent ability to attract and retain capable employees.
- Develops and maintains an effective program of rewards to employees who recruit new members of the staff.
- Displays excellent skills in overseeing employee records.
- Effectively manages relations with union and collective bargaining representatives.
- Is consistently available to meet with coworkers on a one-to-one basis to discuss concerns.
- Keeps abreast of the latest federal and state regulations affecting personnel.
- Keeps the employee handbook current, adapting it to changing conditions as necessary.
- Maintains appropriate controls over the privacy of employee information.
- Works closely with the executive team in keeping personnel costs under control.
- Works well with managers and supervisors to set up effective recruiting programs.

Needs Improvement

- Is not always easily accessible to coworkers on a one-on-one basis.
- Must assist managers in developing and running employee orientation programs.
- Must coordinate personnel policies with in-house counsel.
- Must maintain better control over the privacy of employee information.
- Needs to better demonstrate ability to attract and retain capable employees.
- Needs to improve ability to effectively manage relations with union and collective bargaining representatives.
- Needs to improve skills in overseeing employee records.
- Needs to keep more current on workplace regulations affecting employees.
- Needs to keep the employee handbook current, adapting it to changing conditions as necessary.
- Needs to work closely with the executive team in keeping personnel costs under control.
- Needs to work more effectively with managers and supervisors to set up effective recruiting programs.
- Should strive to develop and maintain an effective program of rewards to employees who recruit new members of the staff.

Unsatisfactory

- Demonstrates a lack of knowledge and understanding of laws affecting the workplace.
- Does not adequately maintain and oversee employee records.

- Does not coordinate personnel policies with in-house counsel.
- Does not encourage head-to-head meetings with coworkers.
- Fails to demonstrate ability to attract and retain capable employees.
- Fails to maintain necessary control over the privacy of employee information.
- Has demonstrated lack of attention to assisting managers in developing and running employee orientation programs.
- Has failed to develop and maintain an effective program of rewards for employees who recruit new members of the staff.
- Has failed to keep the employee handbook current, adapting it to changing conditions as necessary.
- Has not demonstrated ability to effectively manage relations with union and collective bargaining representatives.
- Has not shown ability to work closely with the executive team in keeping personnel costs under control.
- Has not shown ability to work more effectively with managers and supervisors to set up effective recruiting programs.

In-House Training Staff

Key Verbs

demonstrates
maintains

Key Nouns and Adjectives

advancement	promotion	technology
computer based	records	training
orientation		

Meets or Exceeds

- Demonstrates ability to anticipate training needs based on upcoming technical, sales, and marketing programs.
- Keeps current on changing needs for training in the organization.
- Keeps staffers aware of available training programs through newsletters, catalogs, and e-mail notifications.
- Maintains accurate records of training programs to track available skills of employees.
- Makes excellent use of available technology and tools to conduct training.
- Makes excellent use of in-house training staff when appropriate to closely match educational programs to organizational needs.
- Works closely with human resources department to develop orientation training for new employees.
- Works well with human resources department to coordinate training accomplishments with employee advancement and bonuses.
- Works well with MIS staff to develop and maintain computer-based training programs.

Needs Improvement

- Needs to be more creative and imaginative when developing in-house training.
- Needs to coordinate with human resources department to link training accomplishments to employee advancement and bonuses.
- Needs to keep current on changing needs for training in the organization.

- Needs to keep staffers aware of available training programs through newsletters, catalogs, and e-mail notifications.
- Needs to maintain accurate records of training programs to track available skills of employees.
- Needs to make better use of available technology and tools to conduct training.
- Should strive to better demonstrate ability to anticipate training needs based on upcoming technical, sales, and marketing programs.
- Should strive to work better with MIS staff to develop and maintain computer-based training programs.
- Should work more closely with human resources department to develop orientation training for new employees.

Unsatisfactory

- Does not keep current on changing needs for training in the organization.
- Does not keep staffers aware of available training programs through newsletters, catalogs, and e-mail notifications.
- Fails to demonstrate ability to anticipate training needs based on upcoming technical, sales, and marketing programs.
- Fails to establish an effective in-house instructional program.
- Fails to maintain accurate records of training programs to track available skills of employees.
- Fails to make good use of available technology and tools to conduct training.

- Has not demonstrated ability to work closely with human resources department to develop orientation training for new employees.
- Has not displayed capacity to coordinate with human resources department to link training accomplishments to employee advancement and bonuses.
- Has not shown ability to work well with MIS staff to develop and maintain computer-based training programs.

In-House Travel Coordinator

Key Verbs

demonstrates
displays
negotiates

Key Nouns

delays	labor disruptions	travel costs
discounts	outsourcing	travel risks
incentives	policies	travel suppliers
insurance coverage	safety	trends
Internet	security	

Meets or Exceeds

- Demonstrates ability to get the best prices for travel.
- Demonstrates keen understanding of the proper role of travel in fulfilling the mission statement.
- Demonstrates willingness to outsource travel needs when necessary.

- Displays dedication to keeping travel costs within the budget.
- Keeps current on changes in airline industry, including fare trends and possible labor disruptions.
- Keeps employees informed about changes and delays in trips underway.
- Keeps the employee handbook up-to-date on current policies for business travel.
- Keeps up-to-date on changing trends in travel.
- Makes excellent use of the Internet in researching and booking travel.
- Makes excellent use of discounts and travel incentives that are available to company.
- Makes travelers aware of destinations that might present risks to safety.
- Makes use of excellent computer skills to get best possible travel information.
- Negotiates advantageous contracts with travel suppliers and agencies.
- Negotiates reduced rates with travel suppliers for air and rental car usage.
- Works closely with human resources department to train new employees on organizational guidelines for business travel.
- Works closely with other departments in search of ways to reduce travel costs.
- Works with hotel companies to obtain discounted rates for company travel.
- Works with legal department to obtain and keep current appropriate insurance coverage for employees on business trips.

Needs Improvement

- Does not keep current on changing conditions in the air travel market.
- Does not take advantage of incentives and discounts that would be of benefit to the organization.
- Must keep current on changes in airline industry, including fare trends and possible labor disruptions.
- Must keep the employee handbook up-to-date on current policies for business travel.
- Must learn to work closely with other departments in search of ways to reduce travel costs.
- Must work with legal department to obtain and keep current appropriate insurance coverage for employees on business trips.
- Needs to be willing to outsource travel needs if necessary.
- Needs to demonstrate ability to get the best prices for travel without sacrificing security.
- Needs to do a better job of keeping up-to-date on changing trends in travel.
- Needs to improve use of computer to get best possible travel information.
- Needs to keep travel costs within the budget.
- Needs to make better use of computer to keep up-to-date on travel information.
- Needs to make staffers aware of destinations and sites that might be travel risks.
- Needs to work closely with legal department in obtaining and maintaining appropriate insurance coverage for employees.
- Needs to work more closely with human resources

department to train new employees on organizational guidelines for business travel.

- Should strive to demonstrate understanding of the proper role of travel in fulfilling the mission statement.
- Should strive to keep employees informed about changes and delays in trips underway.
- Should strive to negotiate more advantageous contracts with travel suppliers and agencies.
- Should strive to negotiate reduced rates with travel suppliers for air and rental car usage.
- Should work with hotel companies to obtain discounted rates for company travel.

Unsatisfactory

- Does not have an understanding of the proper role of travel in fulfilling the mission statement.
- Fails to keep current on changes in airline industry, including fare trends and possible labor disruptions.
- Fails to keep travel costs within the budget.
- Fails to keep up-to-date on changing trends in travel.
- Fails to make adequate use of computer as a tool for trip and travel information.
- Fails to work closely with human resources department to train new employees on organizational guidelines for business travel.
- Fails to work closely with legal department in obtaining and maintaining appropriate insurance coverage for employees.
- Has failed to demonstrate ability to outsource travel needs if necessary.

- Has failed to keep employees informed about changes and delays in trips underway.
- Has failed to keep the employee handbook up-to-date on current policies for business travel.
- Has failed to make staffers aware of destinations and sites that might be travel risks.
- Has failed to negotiate more advantageous contracts with travel suppliers and agencies.
- Has failed to show ability to use computer to get best possible travel information.
- Has failed to work with hotel companies to obtain discounted rates for company travel.
- Has not demonstrated ability to make use of incentives and discounts of value to the organization.
- Has not demonstrated ability to work with legal department to obtain and keep current appropriate insurance coverage for employees on business trips.
- Has proved unable to negotiate reduced rates with travel suppliers for air and rental car usage.
- Has shown no ability to use the Internet in researching and booking travel.

Legal Services Personnel

Key Verbs

delivers
demonstrates
protects
represents

Key Nouns

advice	mission statement	regulators
laws	missteps	representation
legislators		

Meets or Exceeds

- Ably protects the company from legal missteps.
- Ably represents the organization in meetings with legislators and regulators.
- Is always available for quick advice to managers.
- Delivers excellent legal representation in all matters.
- Demonstrates a commitment to the core values embodied in the mission statement.
- Demonstrates the ability to obtain expert outside counsel when appropriate.
- Is readily available to managers and other staffers to provide legal advice.
- Keeps current on changes to laws, regulations, and legal rulings that affect the organization.
- Keeps managers and supervisors up-to-date on changes in laws and regulations.
- Provides important training and advice to supervisors about personnel matters.
- Represents the organization ably in all legal matters.
- Works with the bar association and the legal community in search of new employees to recruit.

Needs Improvement

- Is not up-to-date on laws and regulations affecting the company.
- Needs to be more readily available to managers and other staffers to provide legal advice.
- Needs to better represent the organization in meetings with legislators and regulators.
- Needs to demonstrate a commitment to the core values embodied in the mission statement.
- Needs to demonstrate ability to recruit new employees for the department.
- Needs to develop proactive programs to protect the company from legal missteps.
- Needs to develop programs to provide important training and advice to supervisors about personnel matters.
- Needs to improve ability to represent the organization in all legal matters.
- Should be consistently available for quick advice to managers.
- Should keep managers and supervisors up-to-date on changes in laws and regulations.

Unsatisfactory

- Cannot be counted on to be consistently available for quick advice to managers.
- Does not demonstrate a commitment to the core values embodied in the mission statement.
- Does not keep current with laws and regulations affecting the organization.
- Does not represent the organization well in meetings with legislators and regulators.

- Fails to develop proactive programs to protect the company from legal missteps.
- Fails to keep managers and supervisors up-to-date on changes in laws and regulations.
- Has demonstrated propensity to misinterpret rulings and regulations resulting in costly mistakes for the company.
- Has failed to demonstrate ability to ably represent the organization in all legal matters.
- Has failed to effectively recruit new employees from the legal community.
- Has not demonstrated ability to develop programs to provide important training and advice to supervisors about personnel matters.
- Is often not readily available to managers and other staffers to provide legal advice.

Mailroom Supervisor

Key Verbs

demonstrates
develops
displays
manages

Key Nouns

delivery
logic

order
shipping companies

shipping costs
technology

Meets or Exceeds

- Keeps mailroom in an orderly and logical manner.
- Demonstrates understanding of new trends in technology and tools.
- Makes excellent use of available technologies and tools.
- Works closely with other departments to find ways to reduce shipping costs
- Develops and maintains programs to help the organization save money on shipping.
- Displays excellent skills in negotiating contracts with shipping companies.
- Manages the timely delivery of internal mail.

Needs Improvement

- Needs to demonstrate understanding of new trends in technology and tools.
- Needs to develop and maintain programs to help the organization save money on shipping.
- Needs to improve the interoffice circulation of correspondence.
- Needs to improve the timely delivery of internal mail.
- Should make better use of available technologies and tools.
- Should strive to improve skills in negotiating contracts with shipping companies.
- Should work more closely with other departments to find ways to reduce shipping costs.

Unsatisfactory

- Does not handle the delivery of mail or interoffice correspondence in a timely manner.
- Does not make good use of available technologies and tools.
- Fails to work closely with other departments to find ways to reduce shipping costs.
- Has failed to demonstrate understanding of new trends in technology and tools.
- Has failed to improve the timely delivery of internal mail.
- Has not demonstrated ability to develop and maintain programs to help the organization save money on shipping.
- Shows inadequate skills in negotiating contracts with shipping companies.

Maintenance and Janitorial

Key Verbs

demonstrates
displays
oversees
supervises

Key Nouns

capital expenditures   equipment and tools   outsourcing
cleanliness   maintenance   pilferage

Meets or Exceeds

- Demonstrates strong understanding of the organization's products and services.
- Displays great pride in the quality and condition of the workplace.
- Has decreased the amount of theft and pilferage substantially.
- Has demonstrated ability to outsource services effectively when appropriate.
- Keeps current on new tools and technology for the workplace.
- Keeps maintenance equipment and tools in top-notch condition.
- Keeps within budget.
- Oversees the maintenance of company tools and equipment exceptionally well.
- Supervises staff effectively.
- Working with security office, developed an effective program to guard against pilferage.
- Works closely with executives and purchasing department to anticipate the need for major capital expenditures and repairs.
- Works closely with other departments to monitor maintenance needs and performance.

Needs Improvement

- Has not shown ability to outsource when necessary.
- Is inconsistent in keeping the workplace environment at an acceptable level of cleanliness.
- Must better control and eliminate theft and pilferage.

- Must improve ability to keep company equipment and tools in acceptable condition.
- Must improve the level of communication with staff.
- Needs to improve ability to maintain close control and scrutiny over company equipment and tools.
- Needs to improve understanding of the organization's products and services.
- Needs to improve working relationship with executives and purchasing department to anticipate the need for major capital expenditures and repairs.
- Needs to keep within budget for ordinary operations.
- Needs to work more closely with other departments to monitor maintenance needs and performance.
- Should keep more current on new tools and technology for the workplace.

Unsatisfactory

- Displays inconsistent effort in keeping the workplace environment at an acceptable level of cleanliness.
- Does not communicate well with staff.
- Does not keep adequate control over company tools and equipment.
- Does not keep current on new tools and technology for the workplace.
- Fails to anticipate major capital expenditures and repairs.
- Fails to control and eliminate theft and pilferage.
- Fails to maintain close control and scrutiny over company equipment and tools.
- Fails to show ability to outsource when necessary.
- Has allowed company tools and equipment to deteriorate

to an unacceptable condition.
- Has failed to adequately manage staff.
- Has failed to improve the level of communication with staff.
- Has failed to improve understanding of the organization's products and services.
- Has failed to keep within budget for ordinary operations.
- Has not shown ability to keep company equipment and tools in acceptable condition.
- Has not shown ability to work closely with other departments to monitor maintenance needs and performance.
- Has proved unable to establish appropriate and effective working relationship with executives and purchasing department to anticipate the need for major capital expenditures and repairs.
- Has shown lack of care and sloppiness in keeping the office environment at an acceptable level of cleanliness.
- Theft and pilferage has increased.

Marketing Director

Key Verbs

| communicates | demonstrates | displays |
| coordinates | develops | |

Key Nouns

| consultant | market research | strategic planning |
| Internet | pricing strategies | trends |

Meets or Exceeds

- Communicates changing trends in the market to sales force.
- Coordinates with MIS department and outside consultant to develop Internet presence.
- Demonstrates strong understanding of market research techniques and tools.
- Demonstrates success in conveying the company's message to the appropriate audience.
- Develops and maintains an effective presence on the Internet.
- Develops effective segmentation strategies for sales campaigns.
- Displays strong strategic planning for trade shows and special presentations.
- Does an excellent job of coordinating marketing efforts with public relations and sales staffs.
- Works closely with meeting planners to develop strategies for trade shows.
- Works closely with sales staff on pricing strategies.
- Works well with other departments in developing marketing plans.

Needs Improvement

- Must develop more effective segmentation strategies for sales campaigns.
- Must work more closely with sales staff on pricing strategies.
- Needs to better communicate changing trends in the market to sales force.
- Needs to better identify the suitable audience to convey the

company's message.

- Needs to coordinate with MIS department and outside consultant to develop Internet presence.
- Needs to develop strong strategic planning for trade shows and special presentations.
- Needs to improve ability to work with other departments in developing marketing plans.
- Needs to improve understanding of market research techniques and tools.
- Should strive to develop and maintain an effective presence on the Internet.
- Should strive to improve coordination of marketing efforts with public relations and sales staffs.
- Should work more closely with meeting planners to develop strategies for trade shows.

Unsatisfactory

- Does not communicate the company's message to the appropriate audience.
- Does not develop effective segmentation strategies for sales campaigns.
- Does not show evidence of understanding of market research techniques and tools.
- Fails to communicate changing trends in the market to sales force.
- Fails to work closely with sales staff on pricing strategies.
- Has failed to demonstrate ability to work closely with meeting planners to develop strategies for trade shows.
- Has failed to improve coordination of marketing efforts with public relations and sales staffs.

- Has not developed and maintained an effective presence on the Internet.
- Has not shown ability to work with other departments in developing marketing plans.
- Has proved unable to develop strong strategic planning for trade shows and special presentations.
- Unable to demonstrate ability to coordinate with MIS department and outside consultant to develop Internet presence.

Meeting Planner

Key Verbs

demonstrates
displays
negotiates

Key Nouns

contracts	meetings	teleconferences
conventions	presentation aids	tools
details	resources	travel providers
facilities	scheduling tools	travel requirements
meeting facilities	technologies	Web-based conferences

Meets or Exceeds

- Can be depended on to get the appropriate presentation aids requested.
- Demonstrates excellent ability to focus on the details of a complex meeting.

- Demonstrates excellent skills in following up to ensure availability of promised facilities and resources for meetings.
- Demonstrates excellent understanding of new tools and technologies for meetings.
- Displays excellent skills in securing necessary services and equipment for meetings, and following up to ensure their delivery.
- Displays great skill in matching groups and location.
- Has consistently demonstrated ability to negotiate advantageous contracts with travel and meeting facility providers.
- Has demonstrated consistent ability to negotiate discounts from travel providers and meeting facilities.
- Has developed an effective program of teleconferences and Web-based conferences, saving the organization substantial travel costs.
- Is a proven master of complex details.
- Is meticulous in research about facilities and resources for meetings, conventions, and presentations.
- Keeps current on new trends in meeting planning and travel requirements.
- Makes excellent use of available technologies and tools for meeting plans.
- Makes excellent use of computerized project planning and scheduling tools.
- Makes good use of travel trade shows to research meeting sites and negotiate advantageous deals.
- Performs exceptional research on meeting sites and facilities to assist departments in decision-making.
- Works closely with convention and visitors bureaus to

seek incentives and special offerings.

- Works closely with MIS and other departments to facilitate teleconferences and Web-based conferences to avoid unnecessary travel.
- Works well with other departments in assessing needs for meetings and conventions.

Needs Improvement

- Has not consistently arranged for appropriate presentation aids.
- Is sometimes overwhelmed as the complexity of a task increases.
- Must make better use of available technologies and tools for meeting plans.
- Needs to become more meticulous in research about facilities and resources for meetings, conventions, and presentations.
- Needs to better negotiate discounts from travel providers and meeting facilities.
- Needs to follow up consistently to ensure availability of promised facilities and resources for meetings.
- Needs to demonstrate ability to negotiate advantageous contracts with travel and meeting facility providers.
- Needs to develop an effective program of teleconferences and Web-based conferences, saving the organization substantial travel costs.
- Needs to improve cooperation and planning with other departments in assessing needs for meetings and conventions.
- Needs to improve research on meeting sites and facilities

to assist departments in decision-making.
- Needs to improve understanding of new tools and technologies for meetings.
- Needs to keep current on new trends in meeting planning and travel requirements.
- Needs to learn skills to avoid becoming overwhelmed by the complexity of tasks.
- Needs to make use of travel trade shows to research meeting sites and negotiate advantageous deals.
- Should strive to improve use of computerized project planning and scheduling tools.
- Should work more closely with MIS and other departments to facilitate teleconferences and Web-based conferences to avoid unnecessary travel.
- Should work to become better at securing necessary services and equipment for meetings, and following up to ensure their delivery.
- Should work with convention and visitors bureaus to seek incentives and special offerings.

Unsatisfactory

- Does not demonstrate understanding of new tools and technologies for meetings.
- Fails to demonstrate consistent ability to secure necessary services and equipment for meetings, and to follow up to ensure their delivery.
- Fails to keep current on new trends in meeting planning and travel requirements.
- Fails to make good use of available technologies and tools for meeting plans.

- Fails to perform meaningful research on meeting sites and facilities to assist departments in decision-making.
- Fails to work closely with MIS and other departments to facilitate teleconferences and Web-based conferences to avoid unnecessary travel.
- Has been unable to demonstrate ability to negotiate advantageous contracts with travel and meeting facility providers.
- Has been unable to improve cooperation and planning with other departments in assessing needs for meetings and conventions.
- Has consistently become overwhelmed by complex tasks and details.
- Has not demonstrated appropriate skills in research about facilities and resources for meetings, conventions, and presentations.
- Has failed to consistently follow up to ensure availability of promised facilities and resources for meetings.
- Has failed to display ability to use computerized project planning and scheduling tools.
- Has not been able to negotiate discounts from travel and meeting facility providers.
- Has not consistently arranged for appropriate presentation aids.
- Has not made use of travel trade shows to research meeting sites and negotiate advantageous deals.
- Has not taken advantage of convention and visitors bureaus to seek incentives and special offerings.
- Has proved unable to develop an effective program of teleconferences and Web-based conferences in order to save the organization substantial travel costs.

Public Relations/Public Information

Key Verbs

conducts   displays   produces

demonstrates   maintains   promotes

develops

Key Nouns

contacts

Internet

media

societies

Meets or Exceeds

- Demonstrates a strong commitment to the mission statement in all actions.
- Develops excellent contacts with area media to promote the products and services of the organization.
- Displays an excellent understanding of tools and technologies appropriate to the job.
- Has a manner that is approachable but professional.
- Has produced an effective organizational plan for dealing with media inquiries.
- In cooperation with training staff, conducts training sessions on dealing with the press.
- Is always up-to-date on company products, services, and programs.
- Maintains membership in appropriate professional societies and community service groups to promote the organization's mission.

- Treats the press with cautious respect.
- Where appropriate, is careful to get approval from a department head before information is released.
- Works closely with marketing department to promote the organization in the media.
- Works closely with other departments in developing and maintaining a presence on the Internet for promotion and sales.

Needs Improvement

- Does not always display a professional attitude when representing the company.
- Does not keep current on products, services, and happenings in the company.
- Is not always accessible to the press.
- Needs to demonstrate a strong commitment to the mission statement in all actions.
- Needs to develop and conduct training sessions on dealing with the press, in cooperation with training staff.
- Needs to improve contacts with area media to promote the products and services of the organization.
- Needs to work to better display an understanding of tools and technologies appropriate to the job.
- Should develop an effective organizational plan for dealing with media inquiries.
- Should maintain membership in appropriate professional societies and community service groups to promote the organization's mission.
- Should work more closely with marketing department to promote the organization in the media.

- Should work more closely with other departments in developing and maintaining a presence on the Internet for promotion and sales.
- Sometimes releases information before appropriate approval is given from department heads.

Unsatisfactory

- Displays an antagonistic attitude toward the press.
- Does not demonstrate a strong commitment to the mission statement in all actions.
- Does not display an understanding of tools and technologies appropriate to the job.
- Has demonstrated propensity to release wrong or misleading information.
- Has failed to develop and conduct training sessions on dealing with the press, in cooperation with training staff.
- Has failed to improve contacts with area media to promote the products and services of the organization.
- Has failed to work closely with other departments in developing and maintaining a presence on the Internet for promotion and sales.
- Has not demonstrated ability to work with marketing department to promote the organization in the media.
- Has not maintained membership in appropriate professional societies and community service groups to promote the organization's mission.
- Has proved unable to develop an effective organizational plan for dealing with media inquiries.

Purchasing Agent

Key Verbs

coordinates   displays   seeks
demonstrates   negotiates

Key Nouns

budgets   inventory   trade shows
contracts   spreadsheets   warehouse
databases   stockroom

Meets or Exceeds

- Attends trade shows and conferences to learn about new products and cultivate new suppliers and contractors.
- Coordinates efforts with warehouse and stockroom to permit just-in-time inventory replenishment.
- Demonstrates excellent skills in assisting department heads in estimating costs to draw up budgets.
- Demonstrates excellent skills in negotiating advantageous contracts with major suppliers of products and services.
- Displays deep understanding of the organization's products and services.
- Keeps executives informed anytime anticipated expenses exceed budget lines.
- Keeps up-to-date on emerging trends and new concepts.
- Makes excellent use of computer spreadsheet and database tools to track expenses and make projections.
- Seeks and obtains appropriate training on materials and services.

- Works closely with other departments to anticipate and plan for expected changes in necessary resources.

Needs Improvement

- Must keep executives informed anytime anticipated expenses exceed budget lines.
- Needs to coordinate efforts with warehouse and stockroom to permit just-in-time inventory replenishment.
- Needs to develop deeper understanding of the organization's products and services.
- Needs to improve ability to negotiate advantageous contracts with major suppliers of products and services.
- Needs to keep up-to-date on emerging trends and new concepts.
- Needs to seek and obtain appropriate training on materials and services.
- Needs to work closely with other departments to anticipate and plan for expected changes in necessary resources.
- Should improve use of computer spreadsheet and database tools to track expenses and make projections.
- Should more regularly attend trade shows and conferences to learn about new products and cultivate new suppliers and contractors.
- Should strive to improve skills in assisting department heads in estimating costs to draw up budgets.

Unsatisfactory

- Does not work closely with other departments to anticipate and plan for expected changes in necessary resources.

- Fails to keep executives informed when anticipated expenses exceed budget lines.
- Fails to keep up-to-date on emerging trends and new concepts.
- Fails to make adequate use of computer spreadsheet and database tools to track expenses and make projections.
- Has declined to regularly attend trade shows and conferences to learn about new products and cultivate new suppliers and contractors.
- Has failed to coordinate efforts with warehouse and stockroom to permit just-in-time inventory replenishment.
- Has failed to demonstrate a deep understanding of the organization's products and services.
- Has failed to improve skills in assisting department heads in estimating costs to draw up budgets.
- Has not been willing to seek and obtain appropriate training on materials and services.
- Has proved unable to negotiate advantageous contracts with major suppliers of products and services.

Receptionist

Key Verbs

displays
maintains
manages
presents

Key Nouns

access	guest register	security
appointments	image	telephone directory

Meets or Exceeds

- Displays an excellent knowledge of the organization and its products and services.
- Effectively manages the organization's online and printed telephone directory.
- Helps maintain the front desk guest register, coordinating collection of information for marketing and security departments.
- Presents a friendly and professional image.
- Professionally manages introduction and dispatch of visitors with scheduled appointments.
- Works closely with security department to control access to the building.

Needs Improvement

- Must demonstrate ability to consistently present a friendly and professional image.
- Must work more closely with security department to control access to the building.
- Needs to devote more attention to maintaining the front desk guest register, coordinating collection of information for marketing and security departments.
- Needs to improve ability to manage introduction and dispatch of visitors with scheduled appointments.

- Needs to improve attitude to consistently present a friendly and professional image.
- Needs to improve knowledge of the organization and its products and services.
- Should strive to better manage the organization's online and printed telephone directory.

Unsatisfactory

- Does not present a satisfactory image or attitude when representing company.
- Does not properly manage introduction and dispatch of visitors with scheduled appointments.
- Fails to devote adequate attention to maintaining the front desk guest register, coordinating collection of information for marketing and security departments.
- Fails to manage the organization's online and printed telephone directory successfully.
- Has failed to demonstrate ability to consistently present a friendly and professional image.
- Has failed to improve knowledge of the organization and its products and services.
- Has not shown ability to consistently present a friendly and professional image.
- Has not shown ability to work closely with security department to control access to the building.

Security Officer

Key Verbs

demonstrates
displays
informs
seeks

Key Nouns

fire	police	technologies
homeland security	privacy	tools
insurance carriers	regulations	
laws	security	

Meets or Exceeds

- Demonstrates excellent skills in anticipating and planning for security issues.
- Demonstrates strong knowledge of laws and regulations related to the job.
- Demonstrates willingness to outsource security matters when appropriate.
- Displays a reassuring presence to employees.
- Informs executives and planners of security needs.
- Keeps front desk and receptionists informed of security plans and procedures.
- Keeps up-to-date on technologies and tools appropriate for the workplace.
- Participates in planning and task forces with area police, fire, and homeland security officials as appropriate.

- Seeks out and undertakes appropriate training on security matters.
- Works closely with other departments in planning for the security of the workplace.
- Works with legal department to coordinate security efforts with insurance carriers.
- Works with personnel, financial, and computer departments to ensure the security and privacy of organizational files and systems.

Needs Improvement

- Must improve knowledge of laws and regulations related to the job.
- Must keep up-to-date on technologies and tools appropriate for the workplace.
- Must work closely with other departments in planning for the security of the workplace.
- Must work with legal department to coordinate security efforts with insurance carriers.
- Needs to become better at handing confrontations in the workplace.
- Needs to demonstrate ability to anticipate and plan for security issues better.
- Needs to inform executives and planners of security needs better.
- Needs to demonstrate willingness to outsource security matters when appropriate.
- Needs to improve ability to work with personnel, financial, and computer departments to ensure the security and privacy of organizational files and systems.

- Needs to keep front desk and receptionists informed of security plans and procedures.
- Needs to seek out and undertake appropriate training on security matters.
- Should participate in planning and task forces with area police, fire, and homeland security officials as appropriate.
- Should strive to display a reassuring presence to employees.

Unsatisfactory

- Does not display a reassuring presence to employees.
- Does not display appropriate knowledge of laws and regulations related to the job.
- Does not display the ability to work with personnel, financial, and computer departments to ensure the security and privacy of organizational files and systems.
- Does not handle confrontations in the workplace in an appropriate manner.
- Fails to keep up-to-date on technologies and tools appropriate for the workplace.
- Fails to participate in planning and task forces with area police, fire, and homeland security officials as appropriate.
- Has failed to adequately ensure against the loss or compromise of organizational files and systems.
- Has failed to inform executives and planners of security needs adequately.
- Has failed to demonstrate ability to anticipate security issues.
- Has failed to keep front desk and receptionists appropriately informed of security plans and procedures.
- Has failed to work closely with other departments in planning for the security of the workplace.

- Has not appropriately represented the organization in planning and task forces with area police, fire, and homeland security officials.
- Has not demonstrated ability to work with legal department to coordinate security efforts with insurance carriers.
- Has not outsourced security matters when appropriate.
- Has proved unable or unwilling to seek out and undertake appropriate training on security matters.

Warehouse/Stockroom Staff

Key Verbs

demonstrates
develops
maintains

Key Nouns

management	supplies	tracking
materials	technologies	warehouse
pilferage		

Meets or Exceeds

- Analyzes usage patterns to anticipate upcoming needs.
- Demonstrates an understanding of the latest technologies and tools for warehouse management.
- Develops and maintains a "just-in-time" ordering system that reduces costs and waste.

- Keeps current on available storage and retrieval systems.
- Keeps materials and supplies in an orderly and organized manner.
- Maintains a close control on materials and supplies, reducing or eliminating pilferage and inappropriate use.
- Works closely with human resources department to develop appropriate training programs.
- Works closely with MIS department to develop and maintain appropriate computerized tracking systems for materials and supplies.

Needs Improvement

- Needs to analyze usage patterns better to anticipate upcoming needs.
- Needs to consider development and maintenance of a "just-in-time" ordering system to reduce costs and wastage.
- Needs to keep current on available storage and retrieval systems.
- Needs to keep warehouse and stockroom goods in a more organized fashion.
- Needs to maintain a closer control on materials and supplies, reducing or eliminating pilferage and inappropriate use.
- Needs to work more closely with MIS department to develop and maintain appropriate computerized tracking systems for materials and supplies.
- Should strive to improve understanding of the latest technologies and tools for warehouse management.
- Should work with human resources department to develop appropriate training programs.

Unsatisfactory

- Does not adequately analyze usage patterns to anticipate upcoming needs.
- Does not demonstrate understanding of the latest technologies and tools for warehouse management.
- Does not maintain adequate controls on materials and supplies to reduce or eliminate pilferage and inappropriate use.
- Fails to keep current on available storage and retrieval systems.
- Fails to work with human resources department to develop appropriate training programs.
- Has failed to produce a plan for development and maintenance of a "just-in-time" ordering system to reduce costs and waste.
- Has not demonstrated ability to work closely with MIS department to develop and maintain appropriate computerized tracking systems for materials and supplies.
- Stores materials in a chaotic manner.

About the Authors

COREY SANDLER IS THE AUTHOR of more than 150 books on business, travel, and entertainment topics. He has worked for more than three decades in communications: as a reporter and columnist for Gannett Newspapers and the Associated Press, as director of public information for an agency of New York State government, and as editor-in-chief of two national business publications. For the past decade, he has been an author and editor of nonfiction books and packaging of other titles through his company, Word Association, Inc.

Among his current bestselling books are *Fix Your Own PC*, seventh edition, from Wiley Press, and the *Econoguide Travel Book Series* from Globe-Pequot Press. You can see his current titles on the Internet at *www.econoguide.com*.

JANICE KEEFE worked for Hearst Newspapers and an agency of New York State government before joining Word Association, Inc., as manager.

Sandler and Keefe also cowrote *1,001 Letters for All Occasions*, published by Adams Media.

You can e-mail the authors at *info@econoguide.com*.